RECLAIMING CONTROL

RECLAIMING CONTROL

LOOKING INWARD TO RECALIBRATE YOUR LIFE

AMY MCMILLEN

NEW DEGREE PRESS

COPYRIGHT © 2020 AMY MCMILLEN

All rights reserved.

RECLAIMING CONTROL

Looking Inward to Recalibrate Your Life

ISBN   978-1-64137-905-2 *Paperback*
        978-1-64137-635-8 *Kindle Ebook*
        978-1-64137-637-2 *Ebook*

For My Ten-Year-Old Self

CONTENTS

INTRODUCTION		11

PART 1.
CHAPTER 1.	PLASTIC PONIES	21
CHAPTER 2.	CONSTRUCTED BUBBLES	31
CHAPTER 3.	NEAT LITTLE BOXES	45
CHAPTER 4.	THIS TOO SHALL PASS	57
CHAPTER 5.	YOU ARE THE BOX	77

PART 2.
CHAPTER 6.	EXACTLY WHERE I'M SUPPOSED TO BE	95
CHAPTER 7.	FREE YOUR FEELINGS	107
CHAPTER 8.	THE UNLOCKED CAGE	125
CHAPTER 9.	DESIGN, TEST, ITERATE, REPEAT	135
CHAPTER 10.	MIRRORS BEYOND OURSELVES	147

FINAL THOUGHTS	153
ACKNOWLEDGMENTS	157
APPENDIX	161

God, grant me the serenity

To accept the things I cannot change,

The courage to change the things I can,

And the wisdom to know the difference.

INTRODUCTION

"Amy, you live in a beautiful luxury high-rise apartment with floor-to-ceiling windows, have a six-figure job that you don't completely hate, and your friends are all here. What are you complaining about?" One of my coworkers, Adam, called me out in the middle of one of my rants about my life spiraling out of control.

What was I complaining about? I asked myself this question as I went home that evening, waltzing through the revolving doors of the Ritz Plaza and waving to the doorman as I waited for the elevator to take me to the seventeenth floor. That night, over a face mask and lavender tea, I made gratitude list after gratitude list, trying to will myself into being thankful for what I had. *He's right,* I thought. *I'm living the good life. I'm selfish and entitled for even thinking otherwise. All I need is some self-care!*

So why did I continue having this unnerving voice inside my head that said I wasn't living life on my own terms?

Observing my life up until last year, I certainly wasn't in control. I thought I was, but my life really was controlled by my job, phone, email inbox, college, the corporate ladder, friends, family, the hustle and bustle of New York City, and societal expectations.

There's the catch—none of those things are inherently bad. Working in technology at a large finance firm, my job had decent hours and decent people. I loved my family and friends. I loved (and sometimes hated) both college and New York. My email inbox and phone are simply tools and technology. There was no active pressure from these external entities, yet I internalized pressure all the same.

Though I had always considered myself mature and independent, I hadn't developed the resources and skills necessary to be an emotionally independent adult and manage my own well-being. Before I knew it, I had become a shell of a person, feeling negative more often than not, simply going through the motions to stay afloat.

I had been in perpetual motion for as long as I could remember, without ever questioning where I was headed. Somehow, along the way, I had forgotten how to take a break. Ever the overachiever, even my free time was spent "productively"— attending events, trying workout classes, volunteering, or packing in as many brunch or dinner dates as possible. These were fun and sometimes energizing, of course, but I didn't allow myself a consistent, active practice of slowing down and recalibrating. When I did allow myself a break, it was usually the mindless, numbing type of indulgence, a result of burnout, or the stressful type of relaxation that was more so procrastination. I had gotten really good at working in sprints, like so many of us, especially in tech, are trained to do.

I realized I couldn't remember the last time I simply had the time or energy to think about my own dreams, desires, or interests beyond what restaurant or museum I was checking out that weekend.

The statistics say I'm not alone:

- A 2019 World Happiness Report revealed that negative feelings, including worry, sadness, and anger have been rising around the world, up by 27 percent from 2010 to 2018.[1]
- A 2018 Gallup poll reported that nearly two-thirds of full-time workers are dealing with burnout at some point while at work.[2]
- According to the National Alliance on Mental Illness (NAMI), young Asian American women ages fifteen to twenty-four have the highest rates of depressive symptoms of any racial/ethnic or gender group.[3]

Everywhere we turn, we can get a boost of "zen" and "self-care" by consuming a green smoothie and a shot of ginger and turmeric or attending a yoga class. So how and why,

---

[1] John F. Helliwell, Richard Layard, and Jeffrey D. Sachs, "World Happiness Report 2019," *Sustainable Development Solutions Network,* March 20, 2019.

[2] Sangeeta Agrawal and Ben Wigert, "Employee Burnout, Part 1: The 5 Main Causes," *Gallup,* July 12, 2018.

[3] Jei Africa and Majose Carrasco, "Asian-American and Pacific Islander Mental Health," *National Alliance on Mental Illness,* February 2011, 6.

with all the lavender tea and face masks, are we feeling more depressed, lonely, anxious, and stuck than ever?

Maslow's hierarchy of needs provides one theory to answer this question. Often depicted as a pyramid, at the bottom are the basic necessities of physiological and safety needs: food, water, shelter, safety, security. Going up the pyramid are the psychological and self-fulfillment needs. The crux of the model is that each level needs to be satisfied before moving on to the next level. The model is imperfect, of course (and throughout this book we'll look at modified hierarchies and other frameworks beyond this one), but it does provide a starting point for thinking about society and human behavior.

The focus on attaining these basic needs has shifted over time, most recently for those of us who come from first- or second-generation immigrant or multicultural families. Our parents (and for some, our selves) immigrated to the United States with the sole need to survive and to provide a better life for our families. Now, many of us have since achieved those basic needs of food, shelter, and safety. With those levels met, we're now left lost and confused with the psychological and self-fulfillment pieces of intimate relationships, friendships, feelings of accomplishment, and achieving potential.

***

Growing up in the Cultural Revolution in China, my mom wasn't getting stuck on a lack of deep and meaningful friendships.

Returning to the United States right before the Great Recession with a family of five, my dad wasn't thinking about fulfilling his own creative potential.

As comedian Hasan Minhaj said, "I think that's the big difference between our generation and our parents' generation. They're always trying to survive . . . but I'm trying to live."[4] Certain habits and mindsets on family, money, work, health, and relationships served us when we were in survival mode. Now that many of us are out of survival mode, it's time to create new habits and ways of thinking.

We've been told a certain narrative our entire lives. Do *x*, *y*, and *z*, then you will be handed happiness and success. As someone from a low-income background, my path was set. All I had to do was work hard in school, get into a good college, graduate with a respectable degree (if you were giving up law or medicine, you'd better study business or engineering), then land a job at a prestigious company. Voilà! There's your golden ticket. That's your yellow brick road.

If you've read or watched the classic story *The Wizard of Oz,* you know that Dorothy is told to go to the Emerald City, where the magnificent Wizard will grant her wish to return home. She's told to "follow the yellow brick road." Along the way, she enlists three companions—Scarecrow, Tin Man, and Lion—to accompany her in hopes of the Wizard granting their wishes of obtaining a brain, a heart, and courage, respectively. Spoiler alert: The Wizard is a fraud—a

---

[4] *Patriot Act,* "Hasan Hears Hot Takes From The Audience | Deep Cuts | Patriot Act with Hasan Minhaj | Netflix," December 19, 2019, video, 19:11.

humbug—and can't grant their wishes. Dorothy and her three friends then rely on each other and the journey itself to realize that they had the answers to their deepest desires within them all along.

I grew up thinking that one day I would take control and figure out my life. People told me I just had to put my head down for at least two years. After making x amount of money (I never quite figured out how much would be enough), I could quit and travel the world, doing my own thing (I'd figure out what "my own thing" was then, right?). If I continued to be responsible in my twenties (I had read Dr. Meg Jay's *The Defining Decade: Why Your Twenties Matter—And How to Make the Most of Them Now* and knew my twenties mattered, after all), surely I'd achieve my dream life one day!

We forget that *one day* will never come unless it turns into *today*.

My problem was that I couldn't live my dream life even if I wanted to because I didn't give myself permission to wonder what that might be. I lacked clarity and vision for myself, remaining stuck in states of depression or anxiety.

Sure, I took on the dreams of others and what society labeled as success. Since I moved to the United States, the Land of Opportunity, from China when I was ten years old, my vision had always been on the next steps I had to take to provide a better life for myself and my family. Not because my parents expected me to, but because I expected myself to.

While living in China, my family lived in gated communities with multiple housekeepers. After moving to Virginia, my family cleaned houses together every weekend to make ends meet. Being extremely aware of the power of money from a young age, soon my top priority in making decisions was financial security. When I got to college, everyone who was anyone seemed to be pursuing finance, consulting, or tech, so I followed suit.

I dived into achieving the myth of the American dream, and in turn forgot how to have dreams of my own.

Along the way, I realized that the Emerald City wasn't so shiny after all. Only when I found the courage to surround myself with people outside of my constructed bubbles did I realize that *I had the answers inside me all along.* And I'm here, as a friend, telling you that you can do the same.

PART 1

CHAPTER 1

PLASTIC PONIES

---

con·trol /kən'trōl/ noun. the power to influence or direct people's behavior or the course of events.

–THE OXFORD ENGLISH DICTIONARY

"Close your eyes and take a deep breath as you find a comfortable seated position." I listen to these words while crossing the street, navigating masses of people and honking cars as I make my daily commute across Manhattan.

As I walk, I follow along with the breathing exercises and observe my thoughts: *Is everyone else with headphones on listening to music or podcasts? Wow, I love that coat. I hate when random droplets fall on my head and it's not raining. Oops, I'm supposed to be focused on my breath.*

After the ten-minute meditation ends, I switch to a playlist called "Awake," which is filled with motivating songs to start my day. The second of the five songs in this playlist is "Rise Up" by Andra Day. The first line includes a phrase about how you're tired of living life on a merry-go-round. Andra then goes on to tell me to walk it out. My steps gain more energy as she says to rise up "unafraid" and to rise up "a thousand times again."

I haven't quite listened to this song a thousand times, but I do listen to it almost every single day I walk to my office. I repeat my meditation and music routine each morning for twenty minutes, right from when I take the elevator seventeen stories down from my Times Square apartment to when I take the elevator twenty-two floors up to my office in Midtown East. I find that I am always much more clear-headed when I take the time to breathe, observe my thoughts, and consciously get ready for the day ahead of me.

Today, June 28, however, is different. I put in my headphones and start to observe my thoughts quietly, knowing this is the last time I'm going to make this walk. Listening to Andra Day's opening line makes one persistent image come to me: living life on a merry-go-round, going up and down, 'round and 'round every single day. It wasn't necessarily the city, or my job, or any of my other circumstances. I had "made it" to the Big Apple, living a dream life, yet I felt exactly that: I was stuck in a dream life, and that dream was not mine. It was like I was sleepwalking, going through the motions, nodding yes to the rat race, feeling helpless to my own dreams of what I would do *one day*.

The merry-go-round image is persistent in my mind and brings me back to the moments that led me to this day.

***

Four months earlier, I had sat by the carousel in Central Park, watching plastic ponies with fixed smiles go up and down, 'round and 'round. I was on a long, meandering walk home from East Harlem, where I spent every Saturday morning mentoring high school students. In a group consisting of a mix of twenty mentors and mentees total, we started each session by gathering in a circle and going around answering the question of the week. That particular day, the question was, "What's a difficult decision you had to make recently?" Lauren, a high school sophomore, answered that she went to sleep instead of staying up late to write her paper. Sahil, a fellow mentor, answered that he had to choose between staying at his job or taking a new offer. When it came to me, I answered that I decided to use my vacation days to go to Costa Rica in April for myself instead of going to visit family in California later for July 4. With almost all of my fellow mentors working in the corporate world, they nodded in understanding and mentioned how precious vacation days were always tricky to prioritize.

I didn't think too much of it as we started the session's activities, but my mind wandered back to this decision as I sat on the bench in the crisp air, watching the same horse go around and around. I felt selfish for choosing to go to Costa Rica over spending more time with my family, even though I knew that I wouldn't regret it. I figured I could afford to spend a long weekend with my family still, so it wouldn't be too much of an issue. I had had my eye on taking a two-week permaculture design class in Costa Rica for ages, and it was finally happening. Little did I know that this decision would spark a series of decisions that would rapidly change the course of my future and that I would get more family time in July alone than I had in the past five years combined.

The night before I flew to Costa Rica, I flew back to New York from a twelve-hour interview with a venture capital firm in North Carolina. Since knowing I wanted to make a change from my current job situation, I was exploring possible next steps and spent the weeks leading up to it practicing start-up valuation and financial projections. Three days after I stepped foot onto Rancho Mastatal in the middle of the jungle, I knew I would be quitting my current job to take a long break. For how long or to do what, I had no idea, but it was the first time, possibly ever, that I was taking full control of my life.

***

Smiling to myself, I take the elevator up twenty-two stories for the last time.

When I get to the office, someone makes a passing comment about how "Amy is quitting to go on an *Eat Pray Love* journey to find herself." I just laugh, responding with how I am excited to take a break and travel for a bit.

What I don't tell her is that I am not taking a short-term journey to *find* myself; I decided to take a life-long journey to *create* myself. To contemplate, design, experiment, and build the person I want to become—day by day, decision by decision. After a whirlwind of being told what to do and an entire lifetime of being on a hamster wheel, I needed concentrated time for freedom and creativity. To recalibrate, to be still, and rise up with a clear heart and mind.

So, yes, I quit my job. I have zero plans for what I'm doing. If you ask, I'll only tell you that I'm going to spend some time traveling with my family. Because truth be told, that's all I know right now. Don't worry, I am not here to tell you to quit your job and travel the world. In fact, I'd highly advise against it (at least for now).

I recognize my immense privilege to be in a situation that allows me to do what I'm doing without being completely irresponsible. I have zero debt, no family to provide for, and saved a decent amount of money from a relatively high salary.

I also recognize that I'm taking an internal journey, not an external one. I don't simply want to switch jobs, move cities, or find new friends. At my goodbye party, a friend asked where my head was when I made this decision. I told her, "It's as if I was sleepwalking, and I finally woke myself up." This is partly true—only after I quit my job did I realize that I had been preparing for this for *years*, which is evident from the reactions of close friends and family. It seemed as if this decision came as a surprise to almost no one except myself. "Oh, Amy's quitting her job? Classic Amy." Or, "Finally! I can't believe you even lasted that long."

***

To *reclaim* something means that **It** was previously yours, and then somehow **It** wasn't anymore. And now you're obtaining the return of **It**. Maybe **It** got lost or stolen, or maybe you gave **It** away or sold **It**. Whatever happened, **It** is not in your hands anymore.

Sometimes, **It** is that shirt you thought you had lost, but then you discover your sister wearing it years later. Or perhaps **It** is a piece of jewelry you had to sell years ago but then happen upon in a pawn shop. Other times, **It** is indigenous land that was stolen, a lush forest that was burned down, or basic human rights.

In this book, **It** is your time, attention, emotions, thoughts, and agency. **It** is control.

Our world is defined by control. Throughout history, wars, bloodshed, sweat, and tears have been created because of power and influence. Control has many levels—personal, familial, communal, systemic, societal, technological. There's physical, emotional, mental, and spiritual control as well. Most of the time, these levels of control are so deeply intertwined within one another that we can't tell the difference anymore.

Take a simple example of the seemingly personal decision of what you want to eat for dinner. If you choose chicken alfredo, do you know why you made that decision? What factors are at play? Perhaps you grew up eating chicken alfredo every Sunday evening, or you saw an ad online for an Italian restaurant, or you're cutting down on red meat, or you opened your pantry and saw that you have pasta and white sauce that you need to eat before it expires. You get the point. You had control over some of those factors, but not all of them. Despite all those conscious or unconscious inputs, you still have control over whether you decide to eat chicken alfredo or not.

Now, magnify that for other types of decisions: college, major, job, city, friends, hobbies. Do you know what factors played into making those decisions? Do you take the time to ask yourself? I mean *really* ask yourself, beyond the surface-level rationalizations that we've all been trained to do. Do you have the space or the tools to know how to listen to yourself if you could?

I found that I didn't. And with that lack of awareness, I had lost control.

You don't have to be aware of every single factor that plays into your decisions, but having a level of reflection can help you gain awareness. With this awareness comes ownership, and with this ownership of decisions comes an internal locus of control.

Attributed to Julian B. Rotter in 1954, the locus of control is "an individual's belief system regarding the causes of experiences and the factors to which that person attributes success or failure."[5] If a person has an external locus of control, that person perceives results as stemming from the environment, other people, luck, or fate. People with internal loci of control attribute success or failure to their own efforts and abilities. One isn't necessarily touted as better than the other, though research has shown that people with an external locus of

---

5   Richard Joelson, "Locus of Control," *Psychology Today,* August 2, 2017.

control are much more likely to experience anxiety and depression.[6] Those with an internal locus of control are also less stressed, less obese, and overall physically healthier.[7]

People often talk about locus of control as if it's so easy to simply take ownership of your decisions, successes, and failures. You either have it or you don't. I found that I was unable to simply embrace an internal locus of control without examining elements of where I came from, what I had been ingrained with, and the systems that pervaded society. I was then able to work with this awareness to make decisions with relative confidence and intention, knowing which factors were within my control, which weren't, and what I could do about it.

***

Plastic ponies, going up and down, 'round and 'round. How was I any different? Going up and down the elevators, 'round and 'round projects and meetings surrounded by other plastic ponies with fixed smiles, all a part of the same carousel.

Hold up. I'm not some plastic pony.

I remember this as my mind keeps coming back to this image, listening to Andra telling me to rise up.

---

6   R Hoehn-Saric and D R Mcleod, "Locus of Control in Chronic Anxiety Disorders" *Acta psychiatrica Scandinavica*, no. 72 (December 1985): 529-35.

7   Catharine R Gale, G David Batty, and Ian J Deary, "Locus of Control at Age 10 Years and Health Outcomes and Behaviors at Age 30 Years: The 1970 British Cohort Study," *Psychosom Med* 70, no. 4 (May 2008): 397-403.

Here I was, thinking I'm the plastic pony. Yet I realize I am the rider, with choices of what to ride. I was so stuck that I couldn't see my freedom; only by surrounding myself in an entirely different environment with people living lives beyond the carousel did I recognize the choices I had made to get there.

I found the fighter within me, walked it out, and decided to move mountains instead.

I chose to get on the carousel, I chose to go up and down, around and around, and today, June 28, I choose to get off.

CHAPTER 2

CONSTRUCTED BUBBLES

The trouble with being in the rat race is that even if you win, you're still a rat.

— LILY TOMLIN

I arrived at Rancho Mastatal after a bumpy three-hour Jeep ride through the jungle in the middle of the night with a new friend, Ruzika, who came with me from the airport. Although we alerted the staff that I would be arriving sometime around 3 a.m., we couldn't find any direction as to where I was supposed to stay. Exhausted, I used the remaining bits of my phone battery as a flashlight and tried opening random doors, only to find that they were locked (I would later find out that the one door I failed to open was unlocked, which would have led to an empty bedroom). Probably a bit delirious at this point, Ruzika and I found a single couch next to the outdoor kitchen, where I took off the back cushions and curled up on the floor. A couple hours later, I woke up to sunshine, a puppy licking my face, and a barefoot man with a gray beard, hippie pants, and a New Zealand accent asking if I wanted coffee. What on earth had I gotten myself into?

***

When I decided to go to Costa Rica to get certified in permaculture design, all I knew was that I was pursuing an interest. I didn't know that I would get a glimpse of what it meant to be *free*.

Sitting in an open classroom made out of bamboo, Scott told us he committed to a desk job years ago after studying economics in college, only to take a road trip throughout Latin America that extended for the next ten years.

Eating her daily diet of mangos, jackfruit, and coconut, Ana shared how she designed apps in San Jose, only to realize that the user experience she was designing didn't quite align with what her body needed at the time.

Swinging on a hammock outside our bunkhouse, Sarah recalled how in her high fashion career in Australia, she witnessed her team bickering for almost an hour back and forth around how yellow the color of a button on a dress should be. At that moment, she knew she couldn't do it anymore.

I thought about the many hours I spent in meetings deciding the equivalent of what color buttons should be. I was working with an online system, not dresses, but the sentiment was all the same.

Unlike Sarah, however, I couldn't pinpoint a specific moment when I decided that I had had enough. My journey instead was a slow-burning cognitive dissonance—a soft underlying knowledge that I wanted something different while never having the courage to do anything about it. It was probably a week after I started my first full-time job when I was already listening to podcasts about people who had quit their conventional corporate lives to pursue something different. Though I listened to these people's stories day in and day out, their decisions never seemed accessible to me. I didn't want to simply quit and travel the world just to travel, nor did I have a successful side hustle that could sustain me, nor did I have a brilliant start-up idea. I felt lost and stuck, simultaneously pulled in a million different directions while feeling empty and blank whenever I thought about what I wanted.

Spending two weeks with over thirty people from all around the world from age twenty-one to seventy or older was the first time in my adult life that I felt surrounded by people who knew how to be free. We were on a ranch in Costa Rica because we wanted to be, not because anyone expected us to be.

How novel it seemed to have conversations beyond how sick and tired you were of your job, how annoyed you were at your boss or team, or to answer, "How are things?" with more than, "You know, same old same old." Fun fact: It wasn't just my coworkers or my friends who had these thoughts. A 2018 Gallup poll reported that over 50 percent percent of employees are unengaged at work; 13 percent of those are "miserable."[8]

I thought finding a new job would be the answer, which led me to explore other positions in tech, product, and venture

---

8   Jim Harter, "Employee Engagement on the Rise in the U.S," *Gallup*, August 26, 2018.

capital. I'm thankful that I went through this process, which gave me the confidence that if and when I wanted a new job, I would be able to get one. It also taught me that hopping to another job wasn't quite the answer. I needed to do a lot of internal work on how to control my current thoughts, feelings, actions, and results no matter the circumstances.

The people I met through permaculture not only lived free lives externally, but internally as well. Many days we started class at 7 a.m. and later had evening sessions of group work or extra learning. It wasn't quite the beaches and waterfalls that my coworkers were probably envisioning my Costa Rica vacation to consist of. In that bamboo classroom, sipping on fresh coffee and eating raw cacao beans to stay awake, we learned about water, soil, fermentation, agroforestry, and composting. With the ranch as a living classroom, we applied the skills immediately.

Externally, our days seemed long and arduous, but we never experienced it that way. Who knows if I will ever use some of the skills I learned? Will I ever need to graft a plant or dig swales? Maybe, maybe not. All I knew was that the low-grade anxiety I learned to live with in my day-to-day life back in New York was gone. To live a life filled with beautiful things you wanted to do and learn—what a thought! With each passing day I soaked in the lives of those around me who were living intentionally, I began to see the possibility that I could do the same.

Living in the jungle with people whose lives were so completely different from mine taught me that I could do something beyond my constructed bubbles of tech, finance, and start-ups. The people showed me there were more possibilities and that these possibilities were possible for me, too.

***

For this to make sense, we'll have to explore how I constructed these bubbles for myself. Ever since I can remember, I've wanted to do something meaningful. I wrote countless scholarship and college essays focused around the theme of "changing the world—one step at a time." I had grandiose dreams of devoting myself to public service. I devoted many hours to teaching English and Mandarin to young adopted girls from China, playing music for those with Alzheimer's, and participating in local government. I spent summers learning about and volunteering to help improve homelessness and urban poverty, public health, and criminal justice. In college, I made sure to study social entrepreneurship and sustainable energy. So how did I end up spending my days at a desk, clicking around spreadsheets to optimize money transactions?

Let's look at the example of Alice, a character that Indra Sofian wrote about in his article, "How Top-Performing College Grads Fall Into the 'Prestige Career' Trap."[9]

From a very young age, Alice is groomed to work hard and told she can achieve anything. She is at the top of her class, the leader of her school clubs, the perfect standardized test taker, the best instrument player, a

---

9 Indra Sofian, "How Top-Performing College Grads Fall Into the 'Prestige Career' Trap." *Medium*, January 21, 2019.

solid athlete, and the one with just the right amount of volunteering experience. From testing to summer programs to college applications, she has ascended the ladder of our status culture and educational system. She's jumped through all the impossibly high hoops and done exactly what today's young high achievers are supposed to do.

I am Alice. Alice is me. Since elementary school or even earlier, we're taught that success is gained through external validation and judgment. We learn that success means getting picked by the team captain, picked by science fair judges, picked by a class vote, picked by college admissions officers. What matters is the final grade, the first place trophy, the first chair seat. As kids, we understand that winning the "Most Improved" medal is a failure, because it's public recognition of how terrible you were in the first place.

In our perfectionist, competitive culture, getting into college is one of the first pinnacles of "success." My parents valued education almost more than anything else but didn't know much about the college admissions game other than that standardized tests were important. My dad made sure I started self-studying for the SAT in sixth grade, but I knew that wasn't enough. I had to take matters into my own hands.

At twelve years old, I dissected books like *What High Schools Don't Tell You: 300+ Secrets to Make Your Kid Irresistible to Colleges by Senior Year* and *What Colleges Don't Tell You, 250 Secrets for Raising the Kid Colleges Will Compete to Accept.* Here's one description: "If you want to raise a kid colleges will compete for, you must act, early and aggressively, as opportunity scout, coach, tutor, manager, and publicist—or be willing to watch that acceptance letter go to someone whose parents did."[10]

Yikes.

I spent hours lurking on forums created for high schoolers to simultaneously brag and shame, breeding grounds for anxiety and plummeting self-esteem. I read the Princeton Review's *The Best 385 Colleges* cover to cover and by my thirteenth birthday, I could rattle off nuanced academic and social differences between any Ivy League, liberal arts school, and public research university.

I learned the rules of the game, and with the privilege of sacrificial parents and outside scholarships to pay for fancy summer programs, extra SAT prep, and expensive extracurriculars, I played well.

Now, Alice is in college. Everything's a lot more freeform: Her schedule is more flexible, and she has a vast amount of choice among courses, internships, positions, clubs, and fields. She's also in a completely new environment. She was at the top of her class in high school, but here she is one of many high achievers. She flounders a bit, changing her major at least once, struggling in some classes, indulging some bad habits.

---

10 Elizabeth Wissner-Gross, *What High Schools Don't Tell You: 300+ Secrets to Make Your Kid Irresistible to Colleges by Senior Year* (New York: Penguin Group, 2007).

Alice doesn't really know what she wants. She has spent her life doing what she is told because she's an achiever. But now that she has real choices, she's scared. What happens if she chooses the wrong major or takes the wrong job? What if she doesn't like her path?

There is no right answer. Alice's life is not like all the tests she used to ace.

Graduating as valedictorian from a small-town Virginia high school was one thing. Living in a first-year dorm with supposedly the best and brightest kids at the university was another. So I did what I was trained to do: I found the prestige game and learned the rules. As if taking a full load of engineering classes wasn't enough for my first semester of college, I packed evenings with internship information sessions and meetings for different organizations.

Maintaining the competitive culture we know so well, the University of Virginia (UVA) had applications for everything. It wasn't enough that we jumped through all the hoops and played the game to get there in the first place. The game continued. You couldn't just declare a major or join any club; you had to apply and be chosen. Because I somehow picked up the rules of the game, I decided to apply for one of the most judgmental, prestige-oriented organizations the university had to offer—a professional business fraternity. I was chosen, and by the end of my first year, I could rattle off strategy and cultural differences between top investment banking, consulting, and technology companies.

Now, imagine: What if Alice could find a career that kept her options open? One that gave her skills she could apply anywhere, that boosted her resume to make her even more employable after college? A career that also paid her handsomely and put her in close contact with some of the smartest and most hardworking people she might ever meet? One where everyone tells her how accomplished she is or nods in approval?

That's the prestige pathway of industries like consulting and finance. That's the promise they make, the allure they create, and the status they symbolize.

Around 30 percent of Yale graduates work in consulting or finance.[11] From Harvard, it's almost 40 percent.[12] Marina Keegan, a 2012 Yale graduate, wrote an essay trying to make sense of this phenomenon.[13] She interviewed several classmates, finding that the narrative was something like this: "Eventually, I want to save the world in some way. Right now, the best way for me to do that is to gain essential skills by working in this industry for a few years."

As Annie, a senior at Yale in 2011, told Keegan, "How can I change the world as a twenty-one- or twenty-two-year-old? I know that's a very pessimistic view, but I don't feel like I have enough knowledge or experience to step into those

---

11 "First Destination Report: Class of 2019," *Yale University, Office of Career Strategy,* 2019.
12 Thomas W Franck, "The Graduating Class of 2017 by the numbers," *The Harvard Crimson,* May 2017.
13 Marina Keegan, "Even artichokes have doubts." *Yale Daily News,* September 30, 2011.

shoes. Even if you know that you want to go into the public sector, you'd benefit from experience in the private sector."

In my experience, the narrative hasn't changed much since Keegan wrote about it almost a decade ago. As someone coming from a low-income background, the financial incentive was real for me. Yet I knew it wasn't simply for the money. I still had dreams of "changing the world," no matter how far off they seemed. I told myself that a foundation in technology and finance would allow me to do anything I wanted, from impact investing to social entrepreneurship. If I truly wanted to set myself up to work in sustainability later, surely gaining experience in the corporate world would only help.

Anand Giridharadas, author of *Winners Take All: The Elite Charade of Changing the World,* discusses the tactics top firms use to target university students. On the *Ezra Klein Show,* Giridharadas described how these companies are excellent at mapping the psychology of being in college and pitch themselves as the new liberal arts.[14] Before, a well-rounded education had to include literature, history, and philosophy. These days, we're told that learning foundational analytical and problem-solving skills through spreadsheeting and PowerPointing will help make impact at scale.

Justifications aside, the process these firms offer is simple and familiar. All you have to do is show up at the information sessions and drop your resume, and they take care of the rest. For those that know the game better, there are strategies and

---

14 Ezra Klein, "Anand Giridharadas on the elite charade of changing the world," September 5, 2018, In *Vox*, Podcast, 01:35:48.

forums on how to secure coveted positions, just like in college admissions. We understand applications because we've been doing it all our life. In this case, companies are wining and dining us—of course we're going to take the opportunity to get to know them better.

Also familiar are the social factors of the process. The firms almost recreate parts of the college experience, having a set class of incoming analysts, training periods, and group projects. Out of the six business analysts who were in my starting class, four of us came from UVA. I lived with my best friend from college. If I simply went with the flow, I could spend my entire work and social life with similar, if not the same, people from school. Blurring the line between graduation and work, starting a full-time job almost seems like another start of the semester, just in a different city. As Giridharadas says, "There is an escalator at these places. And it just moves. All you have to do is get on it."

As long as you know how to play the game, it's easy to get on the escalator.

The firms are brilliant at understanding the anxieties of that age, Giridharadas highlights, "channeling it into 'spend a couple years here' and of course what happens to a lot of people, because inertia is real, is that you stay there twenty years."

Keegan writes:

> "What bothers me is this idea of validation, of rationalization. The notion that some of us (regardless of what we tell ourselves) are doing this because we're not

sure what else to do and it's easy to apply to and it will pay us decently and it will make us feel like we're still successful. Even if it's just for two or three years. That's a lot of years! And these aren't just years. This is 23 and 24 and 25. If it were a smaller percentage of people, perhaps it wouldn't bother me so much. But it's not."[15]

Twenty-three and twenty-four and twenty-five would have mattered to Marina Keegan. She passed away at twenty-two in a car crash, five days after she graduated.

I read Marina Keegan's book, *The Opposite of Loneliness: Essays and Short Stories,* which included her essay exploring the consulting and finance industries, at the end of my internship at an investment firm, right before starting recruitment for full-time positions. Even before classes started in the fall, I had already filled my schedule with company events, "just to explore my options." Grappling with the recognition that I was falling into the validation and self-rationalization that Keegan had described, I explored other options as well. From getting accepted into a graduate design program in England, to almost taking a gap year to travel or experiment in entrepreneurship, I have decision tree after decision tree in my notebook, with every possible scenario mapped out.

When October 31, the deadline by which I had to commit to a company, rolled around, I accepted a full-time offer. I was exhausted from the indecision and pressure, and it was easy to sign my name and say yes to a secure position and salary. Answering the dreaded "What are you doing after

---

15   Keegan, "Even artichokes have doubts."

graduation?" question now solicited approving nods instead of existential anxiety, allowing me to spend the rest of the year in peace and certainty.

Moving to New York City was the natural, next step in the template of prestige and competition I had been following thus far. I was simply doing what I was trained to do. Now in Costa Rica, it was time to unlearn all of that and start again.

CHAPTER 3

NEAT LITTLE BOXES

A person's identity is like a pattern drawn on a tightly stretched parchment. Touch just one part of it, just one allegiance, and the whole person will react, the whole drum will sound.

— AMIN MAALOUF

"What do you do?" she asks, smiling innocently of the man next to her. There are four of us standing in a circle, introducing ourselves. We're at a conference, three weeks after I quit my job to do nothing.

I fidget with my water bottle, pretending to take slow sips as I think of what to say when my turn inevitably comes around. Having just driven across the country, I want to say, *I take road trips and think about life,* or, *I have no idea.*

But I don't. I clear my throat and mumble, "I'm in product management." This answer seems to suffice for small talk, and we move on to the next person. *That's not a lie,* I argue in my head. *The product I'm currently managing is myself.*

I spend the weekend dodging similar questions, including, "Where do you live?" Having moved out of New York and about to spend the foreseeable future on the road, I don't have a straight answer to this seemingly simple question either. I'm intentionally homeless and jobless, a fact I'm not quite ready to share with everyone I come across.

***

I've never had great reactions to the standard questions people ask each other when first meeting.

In college, it was "What's your major?" *Do I explain how I made my own major with whatever classes I wanted to take and somehow graduated with an engineering degree?*

And of course, the classic, "Where are you from?" *Do I get into how I grew up between China and the United States and never really felt that I belonged in either?*

Beyond these normal, widespread questions, I'd also regularly get a more targeted one: "What are you?" Multiracial individuals know this question well. I've always wanted to answer, "I don't know; most days I think I'm human." But I don't, because I always know what they mean.

The Museum of Chinese in America (MOCA) in Manhattan showcased an exhibition by Kip Fulbeck on the "What Are You?" question, titled the *Hapa Project*. *Hapa* is a Hawaiian word for "part" that has spread beyond the islands to describe anyone who is part Asian or Pacific Islander. My sister and I perused the portraits with one little Filipino, Irish, and

Mexican boy catching my eye. Answering "What are you?" in small, chicken scratch, partly cursive letters, he wrote, "I'm a very LitteL boy in 5th grade that has no frandS."

Starting at birth, the world tries to put us into neat little boxes. We're trained to fill in little shapes with number two pencils, defining who we are.

Staring at empty boxes on any standardized test or intake form gave me a mini identity crisis, always having to ask, "Do I check White or Asian?" During times when checking multiple boxes wasn't widely available yet, I ended up checking "Other" every single time, as if my "Other" status wasn't apparent enough. Living in China, my sisters and I weren't able to walk anywhere without being stared at as the three little "hun xuers," translated literally from Mandarin to "mixed bloods."

Moving to Chesapeake, Virginia, only highlighted my Other status even more. I entered fifth grade at an almost all White private Christian school, and China might as well have been a different planet. If asked, "What are you?" I probably would've answered quite similarly to the little boy's museum exhibit. Classmates marveled at my perfect English, whispering "Ching chong" behind me in line and jeering, "Did you wear straw hats and live in huts? I know you were out working on rice paddies."

Every multiracial person I've come across has their own version of creating their own definition of belonging. Elaine Welteroth, previously the editor-in-chief of *Teen Vogue* and author of *More Than Enough: Claiming Space for Who You*

Are (No Matter What They Say), never felt like she fit neatly into boxes of any kind. Her White father and Black mother knew she wouldn't be seen as biracial or White, so they decided she and her brother would check "Black," "presumably some interracial parenting scheme to preempt their mixed-race children from having an identity crisis down the line (if that were possible)." Throughout her childhood, every time she was handed one of those "anxiety-inducing personal information cards in school," she and her brother decided they would "buck the system, challenge racial norms, and defy their parents by checking both Black *and* White."[16]

As Welteroth put it, "To be mixed race in America is to exist in a constant state of in-between. You have access to two worlds and are expected to be fluent in both, yet you never belong fully to either one."[17]

This constant in-between state followed me wherever I went. At UVA, the range of options allowed me the luxury of existing between circles and silos. I chose to exist under labels when they served me, like with engineering school or a business fraternity. It was simply easier to exist in college in groups and labels. You always had people to go out with or to go with to Foxfield (a horse race where no one watches horses race). These external labels cast a charade of belonging; for a moment, I knew where I was supposed to be, who I was supposed to be.

---

16   Elaine Welteroth, *More Than Enough: Claiming Space for Who You Are (No Matter What They Say)* (New York: Viking, 2019), 24.
17   Welteroth, *More Than Enough*, 74.

We're familiar with group dynamics from an early age. One of the most iconic on-screen examples of intergroup relations is *Mean Girls*.[18] Within the first ten minutes of the movie, Cady, the new girl, gets introduced to the cliques. Janis explains, "Where you sit in the cafeteria is crucial, because you've got everybody there. You got your freshmen, ROTC guys, preps, JV jocks, Asian nerds, cool Asians, varsity jocks, unfriendly Black hotties, girls who eat their feelings, girls who don't eat anything, desperate wannabes, burnouts, sexually active band geeks, the greatest people you will ever meet, and the worst. Beware of the Plastics."

While some of these labels have aged poorly since the movie's making in 2004, you'll still see middle and high schools play out these social dynamics. When asked in 2019 what the current labels are, one teen answered, "Soccer boys, The Thespians, Partiers, Hippies, Anime Lovers, Artsy people," while another answered, "Nice and Nerdy Seniors, the lax bros, the popular sophomores, the almost popular juniors."[19]

Visakan Veerasamy, one of the best people I've had the pleasure of meeting on the Internet, expresses how he made a table of his own "because there is no table at the cafeteria for kids who look and sound like us. We have to earn our seats."[20] Born in Singapore to a Tamil family, he speaks the language quite poorly, rendering him an outsider within the Tamil community. Indians from India typically think

---

18 *Mean Girls,* directed by Mark Waters, Paramount Pictures, 2004.
19 Morgan Baila, "How Does *Mean Girls*' Most Iconic Scene Hold Up Today? We Asked 5 Real Teens," *Refinery29*, April 30, 2019.
20 Visakan Veerasamy. *friendly ambitious nerd* (self-pub., Gumroad, 2020), 26.

he's Singaporean, while everywhere else, people assume he's Indian.

Visa reveals how he instantly developed a deep admiration for Bozoma Saint John, based on who she is as a person. Currently the chief marketing officer at Endeavor, Bozoma was previously the chief brand officer at Uber and a marketing executive at Apple.

I remember feeling a similar instant spark with Bozoma when I first saw her walk on stage in sparkly stilettos at the Forbes Under 30 Summit at the Massachusetts Institute of Technology (MIT). Her first piece of advice was the seemingly trite, "Bring your whole self," but for some reason in her dangly earrings and glittering magenta skirt I truly believed the words coming out of her mouth. She gave her backstory and spoke about being born in Connecticut and then moving to Ghana, where her parents are from, when she was six months old, and moving a couple times around Ghana and Kenya before settling in Colorado Springs when she was twelve.

In an interview with the *Financial Times*, she reflected, "I don't know if I'm ever considered a part of the community I'm in. I think I've always felt an outsider, in both places, everywhere."[21] I sat in the audience of almost five hundred women as she said she saw this lack of fitting in to be an asset. "I don't think it's any secret that there's a lack of diversity in Silicon Valley," she told us. "But that to me is actually quite

---

21   Leslie Hook, "'People love the Uber product; they don't necessarily love the brand,'" *Financial Times*, December 6, 2017.

beautiful. It allows me to be fully me because there is no one else to look at and say, 'Oh I should be more like that.'"

At a time when I didn't know what being "fully me" meant, Bozoma's words were inspirational, yet empty. More often than not, I conformed to what people wanted me to be, allowing myself to blend in wherever I was. This behavior started as early as when I first learned how to speak. When talking to my dad, I knew to speak in English. When I turned to my mom, I seamlessly switched to Mandarin. As many mixed heritage and immigrant folks understand, the need to assimilate and blend in (as much as possible) is often an act of survival. When assimilation and code-switching become habitual, it becomes difficult to know who you are without external context.

***

I encountered different aspects of my identity formally for the first time in college through an organization called Sustained Dialogue. We sat in a circle of about a dozen participants, discussing social issues affecting the greater student body. We often framed our discussions around eight dimensions of identity, including ethnicity, race and color, socioeconomic status, sex and gender, age, religion, sexual orientation, and ability status. I still remember the first time I learned the term "intersectionality," a concept I had witnessed all my life yet didn't have the vocabulary for.

The Sustained Dialogue program at UVA was founded by Priya Parker, master facilitator, strategic advisor, and acclaimed author of *The Art of Gathering: How We Meet and Why It Matters*. Before working in conflict resolution and peace processes in the Arab world, southern Africa, and India, she grappled with her own identity when she went to college.[22]

Priya arrived at UVA as a first-year in 2000, "the most racialized climate [she] had ever experienced." Everyone was suddenly asking her, "What are you?" While I was used to this question all my life, Priya didn't quite understand it at first. Coming from two cultural backgrounds, she had never really thought about "what" that made her. She'd answer, "I'm an American? I'm a woman?" until she learned she was supposed to answer, "Biracial; my mother is Indian and my father is White."[23]

The "What are you?" question really bothered Priya. She thought, "Why is that the first question people ask me? Why do they need to know 'what' I am in order to place me?" While she always considered her Indian and European heritage as a part of her, it was never her primary identity in the way that her peers expected it to be. Expanding beyond herself, she noticed that students from different racial backgrounds weren't interacting healthily. She complained to a friend about the lack of opportunity to discuss difficult social issues, in which her friend replied, "Priya, stop complaining. UVA's 'student self-governance' is not just an empty saying; it's the way our community functions. If you see a problem, do something about it." In that moment, Priya realized what

---

22 Priya Parker, *The Art of Gathering: How We Meet and why it Matters* (New York: Riverhead Books, 2018).
23 Priya Parker, "Sustained Dialogue: How Students Are Changing Their Own Racial Climate." *About Campus* 11, no. 1 (March-April 2006): 17.

it meant to be an active and engaged citizen in her community and worked to bring the Sustained Dialogue model to UVA in order to improve race relations.[24]

Through Sustained Dialogue and other student-based efforts like it, I was able to learn not only about myself and others, but also about the relationships among different little boxes the world tries so hard to put us in. Moving beyond a college campus, I realized day-to-day social circles and intergroup relations in New York City were a bit fuzzier and carefully hidden behind thinly disguised veils.

I found college to be a place where the many facets of my identity were allowed to exist, albeit in fragments. Depending on the hour, I could be sustainable Amy, advocating for the environment; fun Amy, going out with friends; corporate Amy, talking to consulting clients; or musical Amy, playing piano or singing. Without the many compartmentalized boxes that my college lifestyle provided, I was washed to one primary identity in New York: my job. For the first few months, I embraced this new monotonous life with beautiful simplicity. I loved coming home after a long day of work, relishing on the couch with the glory of there being nothing else I had to worry about.

It started to bother me when I realized everyone around me had the same primary identity, the one metric that signaled our worth. At any social gathering, the first question someone would ask is, "Where do you work?" Whenever

---

[24] Priya Parker, "Sustained Dialogue: How Students Are Changing Their Own Racial Climate," 18.

I answered, you could visibly see ears perk up and brains checking off the "oh, okay, she's a person worth talking to now" box. I hated that I'd feel a sudden flash of validation and belonging, only to immediately feel the emptiness wash over me afterward.

New York is lauded to be one of the most diverse places in the world, but you wouldn't know it if you didn't try. Though vibrant worlds of fashion, art, and music existed, I couldn't seem to break out of the Midtown crowd, vests and coffees in hand, shuffling like ants to cubicles.

When I noticed this, I actively made it a point to meet new people and went to events, exploring outside my constructed bubbles. I listened to the founders of at-home clear dental aligners, interior design businesses, and cryptocurrency start-ups. I met individuals in clean energy, clean feminine care, and clean fashion. I attended author talks at libraries and art show openings at galleries. These places are where I started to see shimmers of stories that inspired me, like those of the creator of an avatar-based social media platform, the environmental engineer turned perfumer, and the consultant who also took creative writing classes and wrote a full-length novel because, as she explained nonchalantly, "Travel projects required a lot of boring nights at the hotel."

Breaking into the venture capital and entrepreneurship world felt exciting, as I got blinded by disco lights in beautiful, high-ceilinged lofts with hammocks in Williamsburg, or got late-night halal with people who seemed to know anything and everything about the New York City tech scene. After I got over the newness of the people and topics, however, I found the signaling parallel to the same game of competition and prestige I knew so well. This time, the metrics of worth were who you knew, how much money you raised, or how much Twitter clout you had.

Different games, same neat little boxes defining who we are.

***

"What do you do?" It's probably the fifty-second time someone asks me this question in the last three days. I've had the opportunity to practice a different answer each time.

When sharing bits of my story with a new friend, she tells me how her husband responds to the "What do you do?" question with a confident, "Mainly nothing; sometimes I bike or read." While she attributes this confidence to his Harvard University education, inherited wealth, and White male privilege, she stresses how important it was to not be afraid to own what I'm doing.

No longer doing a series of mental gymnastics routines, I smile. "I'm on the road for a little bit, taking a break."

CHAPTER 4

THIS TOO SHALL PASS

From what I've seen, it isn't so much the act of asking that paralyzes us—it's what lies beneath: the fear of being vulnerable, the fear of rejection, the fear of looking needy or weak. The fear of being seen as a burdensome member of the community instead of a productive one.

It points, fundamentally, to our separation from one another.
— AMANDA PALMER, THE ART OF ASKING; OR, HOW I LEARNED TO STOP WORRYING AND LET PEOPLE HELP

Content warning: some strong, visual language about blood

I'm eating breakfast at a diner with my parents when I feel it happening. *Why did I drink coffee?* I lament silently, my heartbeat ringing in my ears. *I know my body can't handle it.* Palm trees sway against the blue sky outside the window, reminding me that I'm in La Jolla, San Diego, a paradise filled with scenic coves and tide pools. *There's nothing wrong,* I assure myself. *You're basically on an extended vacation and there's literally nothing in the world you have to do . . . besides bathe in the insecurities of the life decisions that have led to your homeless, jobless state, of course.* I stop the thoughts there, my tingly hands bunch into fists, and as if on cue, my lungs don't seem to work. My mom leans over to take a piece of my breakfast burrito. Before the tears start welling up, I slide my entire plate to her and excuse myself to the restroom.

The feeling is all too familiar yet never fails to catch me off guard. It's crept up midday at the office, when I've needed to escape to the conference room in the corner that no one goes to, eating a soggy salad alone. It's appeared in the middle of buying arts and crafts supplies.

It's as if I only have limited stores of energy and I'm fighting to survive and keep the limited amounts I have alive. Like I'm treading water—if I stop treading, I'll drown.

***

These feelings regularly started appearing when I was fifteen years old. This was my peak phase with Tumblr, an online microblogging platform on which similarly angsty teens gave me the life motto "this too shall pass." I spent the last couple of months as a high school freshman menstruating non-stop, and this phrase got me out of bed every single morning. Instead of listening to the teacher in world history or calculus, I looked out the window and tried to imagine a reality where I could wear something other than black jeans and not worry about blood soaking through my pants.

I never told anyone what was happening because I didn't know what was wrong and didn't want to be a burden.

Freshman year ended, but the blood didn't stop. At the start of summer, I flew to Chicago for a weeklong service-learning program in law and criminal justice. On the plane, I tried convincing myself that all I had to last was one week and then if it was still an issue, I'd go home and tell my parents. After all, I had survived in silence for the last three months. What could go wrong in the next seven days?

Two days into the program, my group was coming back from grocery shopping and going up the elevator, about to cook dinner together. With each ding of the elevator, I felt increasingly lightheaded and nauseated. The second the doors parted, I vomited into an empty trash can in the hallway. Having been in the sun on our feet all day, the program leader and I determined it was dehydration. That night, I repeated *this too shall pass* as I slept with a towel beneath me, knowing I'd wake up to a bloody mess if I didn't.

I asked to sit out the next day, calling my parents in the morning and telling them I wasn't feeling well. They told me to drink lots of fluids and to get some rest. I mentioned being on my period but didn't want to worry them and couldn't find the words to say anything more.

In the afternoon, I went to take a shower in the dorm bathroom, choosing the second stall to the left. I slowly took off each piece of clothing, feeling weaker and weaker as I stripped to my bare skin. Turning on the water, I closed my eyes and felt the warmth wash over me as the water poured on my face. For the first time in weeks, I felt clean, normal, and almost okay again, until I opened my eyes to a pool of red swirling around my feet with no signs of stopping.

Chunks and chunks of scarlet clots, at least twice the size of tennis balls, poured out of me. Any sense of normalcy faded away, and I slowly crouched to sit down on the cold tile floor. I finally didn't have to smile at everyone and fake being okay.

Is this what a miscarriage is like? Or at least some type of death. I'm dying. I'm going to die in this shower stall, naked and alone, drowned in my own blood. With the water still running, I silently cried into my lap, holding my head to my knees, and prayed for it to stop. After what seemed like hours, I wiped my tears, wrapped myself in a towel, and found a sponge and bleach in the supply closet. I knelt on my knees, one hand trying to stop the bleeding and one hand scrubbing until all remnants were bleached away. I reminded myself, *this too shall pass.*

I still didn't ask for help.

That night when my group came back from the day's activities, we did an exercise called the Privilege Walk. It had been one of the most bonding and trust-building experiences I had done the previous year, so I was excited to reexperience it with a new group of people. The exercise required us to start by standing in a straight line, with everyone holding hands, then to step forward or backward based on given statements. Our facilitator started reading the statements: "If there were more than fifty books in your house growing up, take one step forward." I stepped forward. He continued: "If you have been bullied or made fun of based on something you cannot change, take one step backward." I tried to step back but felt so lightheaded my legs couldn't move. I squatted for the remainder of the exercise, still holding the hands of the people next to me as they gave me soft, encouraging smiles.

The program had a policy that if you couldn't participate for two days in a row, they were required to bring you to the emergency room. My facilitator told me that it was completely routine and I had nothing to worry about—they just wanted to cover all their bases.

Once I checked in at the hospital, the nurse commented on how I looked as pale as the bedsheets. I laughed, telling her how I was losing a bit of blood. "A bit?" she asked.

"Well, perhaps a little more than a bit . . ." I tried to describe what was happening.

Everything after is somewhat a blur. Suddenly, they told me that my heart was beating way too fast, that a gynecologist was going to do a series of tests, that they were testing for internal bleeding, that if I had waited just one more day, it may have been too late. So much for *this too shall pass.*

The doctor called my parents from the hospital. I tried leaning up from the bed, straining to hear what he was telling them, but could only make out, "You should get here as soon as possible." Through the oxygen mask, I whispered, "I love you," to my big sister on the phone because I didn't remember the last time I had told her that. My parents weren't able to get a flight from Virginia to Chicago in such short notice, so they drove seventeen hours to get to the hospital as soon as possible.

I was moved to the intensive care unit (ICU) almost immediately, starting the first of four blood transfusions that I would receive over the next three days. I had lost almost three-fourths of my entire body's blood, with my hemoglobin levels at 3.2 grams per deciliter (g/dL). For reference, a normal hemoglobin level for women is 12.3 to15.3 g/dL.[25] The doctor was shocked I hadn't fainted at all and commented on the sheer amount of mental strength I must have had. I smiled and told him I was indeed a stubborn one.

Every three hours, I had my blood taken to ensure that my levels were increasing. I had a whole team of doctors visiting around the clock: the emergency physicians, the pediatricians, the gynecologists, the hematologists, and the cardiologists. Each morning, the team congregated around my bed and joked I was experiencing *Grey's Anatomy* in real life.

The only thing that stopped the bleeding was the pill, as in oral contraceptive pills. After taking three a day, the bleeding slowed down and eventually stopped. The *Grey's Anatomy* team huddled around and told my parents that I had a "freak incident" and would require in-depth, further testing. After days of bed rest, my mom held my arm and helped me get out of bed to practice walking with me in the hospital hallway, taking step by step with me until I regained my strength. My instinctive reaction to pain is to laugh, so I couldn't stop laughing the entire time I took baby steps down the halls, one side supported by my mom, the other by the IV drip stand. My mom didn't find it as funny, but by the end of the

---

25 "Low Hemoglobin," *Cleveland Clinic*, updated February 2, 2018.

hallway, she was laughing with me as well. On my discharge papers, there were comments that I "never failed to smile" the entire time.

I recovered from this incident by going to Philadelphia, where I studied computer science for the rest of the summer. Burying my head in if-then statements, for-loops, and recursion and running around the quad at the University of Pennsylvania provided a decent escape from the looming unknown that awaited me.

Coming home from summer camp was when I had to face reality again. Taking in a sharp breath, I closed my eyes and replayed the words in my head: "Your appointment with the oncology and hematology specialist is Wednesday, August 17." I scanned the mountain of paperwork, each sheet filled with perpetual lines asking about leukemia symptoms, previous treatment, and one question that haunted me the most: whether I had a lawyer or a will. I was fifteen years old; I had not actively thought of how to manage the affairs around my potential death.

That appointment began a series of tests throughout the fall. The drawing of blood didn't seem to stop. With each ultrasound, I thought about how I didn't think I'd experience the cold jelly on my belly until maybe one day in the far-off future if I were to become pregnant. None of the tests came up with anything, confirming the "freak incident" conclusion.

Simultaneously thankful and annoyed, I tried my best to forget anything even happened.

***

The pill ensured I'd only bleed once a month, but that didn't stop the terrifying thoughts and panic attacks that appeared each cycle. Returning to school my sophomore year that fall, I constantly oscillated between crippling anxiety and foggy numbness. I blamed both on the football player who played with my feelings because it was easier to distract myself with boy problems than address any trauma I had experienced from almost bleeding out.

The same time this stress was happening, I continued my phase with Tumblr, using it as a platform to express these internal feelings that I couldn't talk about with anyone else. I only followed a couple of people I knew in real life and started noticing that almost all of us posted quite depressing things online. We'd laugh and joke in the cafeteria and at the lockers, but none of us would ever bring up anything we had shared after going home from school.

When I started noticing this, I wondered if any of my friends had anyone to listen to them, or if they were simply posting to the void. I knew I used Tumblr as a platform to vent, and it would have been nice to know someone on the other side actually cared. So, I started an anonymous account beyond my personal one and gave it a super cheesy name: ventforhope.

At ventforhope.tumblr.com, anyone could submit a "question" in the ask box, either under your account or anonymously. I described the account as a place to safely vent and know someone is listening to you. To my surprise, it started gaining some traction, and hundreds of people from all over the world started to follow this account and submit vents.

A fifteen-year-old from New Zealand submitted a post that started with, "I've never really done this before but I have no one to talk to, I'm going through a rough stage in my teenage life," then proceeded to write about getting pregnant and feeling completely lost. Another person in Korea wrote, "My friends laugh at me when I tell them about my actual insecurities. They think it's funny and not serious. They don't understand."

I gave hotline numbers and responded with encouraging words when appropriate. Other times, I simply gave a simple acknowledgment and posted the submission. The posting in itself made people feel like they were less alone. I'd often get messages that said, "Hey, thanks for talking to me. I don't really have anyone else."

During this time, I interacted with hundreds of people and recognized firsthand how difficult emotions arise and the helplessness that comes with them. Most of these people, including myself, felt like there was nowhere else to turn.

***

Fast forward to my second year of college, when my friend and I were on the top floor of the library cramming for the three-hour physics exam we had later that evening. Hunched over textbooks and notebooks sprawled out on the table, we pored over problem set after problem set. I sat up, about to walk over to the whiteboard to map out an electric force.

Trying to stand, I found that my heart stopped me from moving. Pain seared me frozen in the wooden seat, with my hands tingling. I scratched the insides of my palms, pressing my fingernails so hard they left marks.

"You okay?" My friend glanced back with his sandy locks, pausing in the middle of writing Coulomb's law.

"Yeah I'm fine, just give me a sec," I managed.

I wasn't fine. My friend insisted on walking me to the student health center, where I promised him I'd see someone if he went back to the library and finished the problems we were working on.

After running through standard procedures, the nurse paused and asked, "Do you have something you're stressed about?"

"Oh, I have a physics exam later, but that's normal. I'm perpetually stressed about school. Everyone is." I laughed nervously, my fingernails still digging into my palms.

She continued her questioning. "Do you have a history of anxiety?"

I think I laughed out loud. "Like actual anxiety? No no, never. Sure, I get anxious like everyone else, but it's not *anxiety*." I felt like the exam had already started, and I was miserably failing.

Everything blurred as I heard the words, "You're most likely experiencing symptoms of a panic attack."

I walked out of Student Health straight back to the library, where I plastered a smile on my face and used my tried and true scapegoat of dehydration to assure my friend that nothing was wrong.

A couple of months later, I ended up in the same spot in the nurse's office. This time she asked, "Do you have any thoughts of harming yourself or taking your own life?"

"Not actively," I crossed my legs tightly, smiling as I kept my voice upbeat. She wouldn't let me get away with that answer. "It's normal to *casually* think about getting run over by a bus, right? I mean, especially if you get free tuition." I continued carefully and laughed at the last part, referencing a widely circulated student myth that if a school bus hit a student, they would get free tuition. She looked up from her notes and stared back, unamused. "I mean, we all joke about it...." I trailed off.

I continued this pattern of denial all throughout college, only seeking professional help when physical symptoms became too much to handle on my own. Apparently, it wasn't normal to have extended periods of chest pain, shortness of breath, hyperventilation, and random bursts of crying.

***

In 2018, a survey from the American College Health Association (ACHA) revealed that nearly three out of five college students experienced a sense of "overwhelming anxiety" at some time, and two out of five "felt so depressed they had difficulty functioning."[26] From 2016–17, more than one in three students across 196 US college campuses reported diagnosed mental health conditions.[27] Furthermore, first-generation and racial minority students showed higher rates of depression and emotional stress compared to their counterparts.[28]

Why are college students so prone to developing mental health issues? Students are already in a state of transition, usually under intense pressure to perform. Throw in lack of sleep, drinking and substance abuse culture, juggling anywhere from five to seven classes, extracurriculars, the pressure of the future and deciding what to do with your life after graduating, usually moving every year, differences in social circles and friendships, increased chance of sexual assault—the list of stressors goes on.

If you're from an underrepresented background, stir in worry over finances, student loans, microaggressions, outright racism, or lack of connections or knowledge of resources. And that's just college stuff itself—not taking into account any trauma brought over from family or past experiences. It's no wonder that college campuses are petri dishes for mental health concoctions.

---

26 "The Deteriorating Mental Health of U.S. College Students: Part I." *Imagine America*, March 2, 2020.
27 Sarah Ketchen Lipson, Emily G. Lattie, and Daniel Eisenberg, "Increased Rates of Mental Health Service Utilization by U.S. College Students: 10-Year Population-Level Trends (2007–2017)," *Psychiatric Services* 70, no. 1 (January 1, 2019): 60-63.
28 Michael J. Stebleton, Krista M. Soria, and Ronald L. Huesman, "First-generation students' sense of belonging, mental health, and use of counseling services at public research universities," *Journal of College Counseling* 17, no. 1 (April 2014): 6-20.

My dear friend Beza, having just finished her sophomore year at a small, elite, private university, also observed this petri dish on her campus, with mental health issues cropping up left and right within her friend group. Coming from a first-generation immigrant family from Ethiopia, she noticed that most of her friends also came from lower socioeconomic backgrounds and from households that never taught them how to deal with their emotions.

After spending her freshman spring semester almost entirely in her room unable to go anywhere, Beza was diagnosed with chronic obsessive-compulsive disorder, anxiety, and panic disorder. With her dad telling her that the diagnoses weren't real and to ignore the doctors, her older sister became her primary pillar of support. Beza couldn't help but think, "Will I always be a burden on somebody?" and wonder if she would ever overcome the helplessness of not knowing how to be self-sufficient.

At the same time, this helplessness stemmed from feelings of isolation and pressures to be self-sufficient. Growing up, Beza felt like she had to figure everything out on her own. She was the one that filled out all her forms, getting herself to college. And once again, she felt she had to face these challenges alone. However, she soon found out that handling it alone wasn't sustainable. She knew she had to confront not knowing how to communicate her feelings, realizing that "it gets to the point where it becomes unmanageable and we can't do it alone anymore."

Beza doesn't know how different threads of identity and context weave into her situation and the larger situation at hand, only that they are very much present. "There are all of these points we're playing. . . . I don't even know where one starts and one ends. The not knowing also exasperates everything."

∗∗∗

We aren't taught to understand, communicate, or even acknowledge mental health as an entity. I remember thinking how radical my high school English teacher seemed when she encouraged us to use our allotted sick days as "mental health days" for our own sanity.

It wasn't until I went on a leadership and identity retreat in college when I understood that *everyone* has mental health, healthy or unhealthy, well or unwell, and everything in between. Our facilitator reminded us, "In the same way we brush our teeth and shower for body hygiene, we also need to regularly take care of our mind's hygiene." It was the first time I heard people talking openly and constructively about issues like depression, anxiety, borderline personality disorder, and bipolar disorder.

Using the sustained dialogue method, we sat in a circle and discussed mental health experiences and how they related to other facets of our identities. I was confident in discussing the other modules, including race/ethnicity, socioeconomic status, gender, and even sexuality, but for some reason I couldn't bring myself to participate fully in this conversation. Ironically, my mouth dried and throat closed whenever someone shared personal examples of anxiety. Hearing others talk about their experiences simultaneously made me feel better and worse. I knew I wasn't alone, yet perhaps I had to finally face that there was something wrong. Each time it was my turn, I'd hurriedly pass along the spotlight, as if I had to prevent a dirty secret of mine from spilling out.

Toward the end of the night, after listening to hours and hours of intense stories, I tiptoed into sharing how I never thought my feelings were legitimate because they were usually sparked from boy problems or school or some other frivolous matter. After I sat back into the safety of silence, a couple moments passed before a member who had been quiet throughout the day started to speak. Floodgates opened about the pressure of keeping up appearances, of being in all the right organizations, of staying on top of every class, only to constantly feel like the weight of keeping up might crash on him any second. He turned to me at the end, thanking me for ignoring the hierarchy of suffering we're trained to embrace and in turn allowing him to be vulnerable and share. My ego wasn't sure whether to be offended or honored that what I shared was considered trivial enough to empower him as well. Activating my inner *Animal Farm*, I couldn't help but judge myself with the idea that *sure, all issues are valid, though perhaps some issues are more valid than others.*

At the time, I didn't know that issues affecting us on the surface level, sometimes in therapy framed as the presenting problem (i.e. the answer to the question, 'What brings you here today?'), are only the tip of the iceberg. Because we're so used to numbing our feelings with distractions or defenses, we often don't even allow ourselves to dig beyond the problems that appear to be superficialities. For example, Lori Gottlieb, therapist and author of *Maybe You Should Talk to Someone: A Therapist, HER Therapist, and Our Lives*

Revealed, initially goes to therapy herself to "just get through a breakup," only to unravel deeper mindset beliefs surrounding grief, change, and freedom.[29]

Post-retreat, I briefly thought about whether I should seek help, but the semester became too busy, and I convinced myself it wasn't a big deal and that I didn't have the time. *Maybe next year,* I thought. *Right now, I need to study physics.*

***

During high school, one of the few friends I knew in person who I also followed on Tumblr was Gabby. I knew we both experienced depression at the time, but we never openly talked about any issues we had; we'd only do so almost a decade later. Whenever she showed any signs of mental distress, people thought she was overreacting and being "annoyingly emotional," to the point that she would believe it herself. Afraid of being a burden, she was paralyzed with fear of asking for help. Over time, her depressive state became a part of the ordinary, so she never thought to think anything was explicitly wrong.

In undergrad, Gabby considered going to therapy but also didn't feel like her situation was "bad enough" to be taken seriously. She finally gave in at the strong encouragement of her boyfriend at the time, thinking she didn't have anything to lose. Slowly but surely, she allowed herself to get over the stigma of therapy and medication and got significantly

---

29 Gottlieb, Lori, *Maybe You Should Talk to Someone: A Therapist, HER Therapist, and Our Lives Revealed* (New York: HMH Books, 2019), 56.

better over time. She realized how stigma had prevented her from seeking treatment and decided to join a mental health advocacy group at her university, thus starting her journey to becoming a therapist.

Around the same time, I was also sensing a shift on my college campus. Though I continued my denial of my personal deteriorating mental health, I couldn't block out what I knew to be true: Mental health was real, as real as the stigma attached to it.

Suddenly, I saw it everywhere. #fightthestigma stickers were slapped all around campus, mental health checkups were available at dining halls, and people encouraged others to seek counseling. I wasn't sure if it was personal confirmation bias, isolated to college campuses, or if society at large was experiencing an overall awakening.

On the surface, the stigma seemed to be washed away. Brené Brown became a household name, and thus we expected ourselves and everyone around us to magically understand how to deal with vulnerability and shame. I conducted research on how to design technology systems to better research and treat college students with depression or anxiety. People started recognizing the importance and validity of mental health all around. *Except did we really?*

***

I carried the "freak incident" with me years later, and it eventually led to a diagnosis of polycystic ovarian syndrome (PCOS) while in college. I had doctor's appointments every single week for a couple of semesters. Along with tracking physical symptoms, my doctor suggested I make regular appointments with Counseling and Psychological Services (CAPS) for students. I didn't want to go. I told myself I didn't have the time or energy to add yet another appointment to my already overflowing schedule. She, however, was adamant, and I thought I'd probably raise red flags if I put up too much of a fuss. I'd later find out that among all racial and ethnic minority groups, Asian American college students are the least likely to utilize professional psychological care, even when actively experiencing mental health issues.[30]

She clicked her pen into the pocket of her white coat, informing me that she'd make an intake appointment for the next day. "There's a huge waitlist, as usual of course, so you're lucky you'll be able to see the specialist at the engineering school right away." I wondered if I was supposed to be grateful for the gravity of the situation that allowed me to skip to the front of the line.

I wouldn't be formally diagnosed with depression until a couple months before graduation, a condition I tried to ignore until I thought I might not graduate. I sat with the dean of students as she gave me a pep talk. "I want you to take a deep breath. You've worked tremendously hard and you're going to graduate." I glanced at the #fightthestigma sticker

---

30 Brandt Kam, Hadrian Mendoza, and Akihiko Masuda, "Mental Health Help-Seeking Experience and Attitudes in Latina/o American, Asian American, Black American, and White American College Students," *International Journal for the Advancement of Counselling* 41 (2019): 492-508.

on her door as she sent an email to my professors without a second thought.

Not everyone in college has the privilege of having administrators as advocates. Beza, looking for resources, had administrators tell her to deal with it on her own, with one telling her that "people have either been able to handle it, or they don't go to school."

Every level reeked of hypocrisy. Colleges and corporations started offering mindfulness workshops galore, yet we never questioned why individuals at these colleges and corporations needed so much meditation. I was designing apps to better research behavior in my classmates struggling with mental health, yet I didn't pursue consistent therapy myself. I wouldn't feel ready to do so until I left the college bubble, yet quickly found out that the entire system around mental health care was as broken as I felt.

Discouraged at every step of the process, from the inquiry to the insurance, I decided to continue to develop my own tool kit. No longer accepting my own passive state, I learned and experimented as much as I could to improve my health.

***

The palm trees continue to sway, now against the purple dusk backdrop. I feel the sand beneath my feet, listening to the waves lap the shore, squinting slightly as the sun begins descending behind the gray-blue clouds. It looks like there's an island in the far-off distance; I can barely make out its silhouette, as it almost blends into the clouds creeping below the horizon. Dogs are playing catch and children are squealing as the smell of salt fills every breath. Everything is slightly damp as the sun keeps setting, creeping behind the cliffs.

I don't tell myself *this too shall pass* like a passive, helpless child anymore. I remind myself that in this moment, I have both the ability to ask for help and the power to transform myself.

CHAPTER 5

YOU ARE THE BOX

―

Why do you wonder that globetrotting does not help you, seeing that you always take yourself with you? The reason that set you wandering is ever at your heels.

—SOCRATES

The staring starts the second I get off the plane, reminding me that the motherland, the country I was born in and spent my childhood in, sees me as a foreigner. Yet something about my foreignness makes me feel at home. Thirteen years of exponential development and revolutionizing technology later, it feels the same. I eat baozi from street vendors, test gel pens at the corner stationery store, and swat mosquitoes away in the damp, gray air. My bare feet pit-patters on the wooden floor, my aunt scolding me to put on straw slippers. Draping over my uncle's black leather couch, the blankets with the pink embroidered flowers still smell like mothballs soaked in chamomile. Sounds of my cousin, now with his own five-year-old, playing the video games he was so enamored with as a teenager still linger in the background. Only when I see the QR codes everywhere, from dog tags to candles to napkins, do I get sucked out of the time warp, remembering that this isn't the China I left behind.

What is most familiar, a feeling carried across the ocean, is the disquieting, nagging sense of internal discomfort. Externally, I marvel at some of the country's most iconic locations, from the mountains as seen on the twenty-yuan bill to billowing golden terraced rice fields. Yet quietly in the backdrop are the sensations of sweat dripping down my neck and the acute stares from never-ending crowds. *Why is everything annoying?* I think. *If I'm going to be annoyed by everything, I might as well have stayed in New York where at least I'd be making money.*

This familiar feeling of discomfort reminded me of a *Saturday Night Live* skit in which Adam Sandler represents an Italian touring company called Romano Tours.[31] Every so often, a customer leaves a review of the tour saying that they were disappointed or didn't have as much fun as they thought they would. Sandler reminds them with great confidence, "Here at Romano Tours, we always remind our customers: If you're sad now, you might feel sad there." The bit then goes through how Romano can provide adventures like hiking, swimming, and zip-lining but cannot make customers genuinely feel adventurous or feel comfortable in a swimsuit. "If you and your partner do not want to touch each other back home, chocolate strawberries will not magically make you want to touch each other in Italy, because you will still have the same bodies and thoughts on vacation as well." Romano Tours will bring you to some of the most beautiful places on

---

31 *Saturday Night Live*, "Romano Tours," May 4, 2019, video, 4:11.

Earth—hiking at the Amalfi Coast, fishing at Sorrento—but "remember, you're still going to be *you* on vacation. If you are sad where you are, you are going to be the same sad *you* you are in Italy."

***

During one therapy session, I sat across the table from the counselor, all smiles. We talked about the topic of novelty in my life and how traveling to new places was often the source of that novelty.

"So, you're comfortable in new situations. What is it that you're trying to escape?" she asked.

"Escape? No no no." I wrung my hands together as I laughed in response. "I just like trying new things! You know, adventure and fun."

However, I couldn't quite trick myself. Call it a classic case of commitment issues or whatnot; deep down, I knew a part of me was addicted to the anonymity, the wonder, and an underlying shifting of discomfort.

To understand illusions of pursuing wanderlust as the cure, we look no further than the wisdom of the ancient classics. In *Letters from a Stoic,* the philosopher Seneca adds to the words of Socrates on travel:[32]

---

32 Seneca, Lucius Annaeus. *Letters from a Stoic: Volume I,* trans. Richard Mott Gummere (Enhanced Media, 2016), 70.

What pleasure is there in seeing new lands? Or in surveying cities and spots of interest? All your bustle is useless. Do you ask why such flight does not help you? It is because you flee along with yourself. You must lay aside the burdens of the mind; until you do this, no place will satisfy you.

On his blog *More To That*, Lawrence Yeo creates an adaptation of Seneca's letter on travel in the form of a viral article called "Travel Is No Cure for the Mind."[33] Yeo's signature style uses illustrations that look like they're stitched together in Microsoft Paint. The article starts by introducing *you*, a triangle-headed individual living a mundane life, often looking to the outside world in far-off lands for adventure. Yeo writes,

> *Travel is the answer much of us look to when we feel the automation of life. The routine of waking up, getting ready, going to work, eating the same lunch, sitting in meetings, getting off work, going home, eating dinner, relaxing, going to sleep, and then doing it all over again can feel like a never-ending road that is housed within the confines of a mundane box.*
>
> *This is* **The Box of Daily Experience**, *and it is the space we occupy on any given day of the week/month/year in which we live our lives. It is what we consider "normal" in the context of an everyday experience, and is the*

---

33 Yeo, Lawrence. "Travel Is No Cure for the Mind." *More To That*, March 21, 2019.

operating system we run ourselves on when we require a sequence of events to default to.

The boundaries of our box define our present-day situation, so when we dreamingly gaze toward the prospects of an exciting future, we look outside of it to experience emotions like wonderment, amazement, and inspiration. Our current box is okay and livable, but the world outside of its boundaries is where our hope really resides.

We think that things outside of our Box of Daily Experience will bring us fulfillment. For some, this could be a new car, a promotion, or often a vacation or the experience of traveling the world. Harvard psychologist Tal Ben-Shahar labeled this phenomenon "the arrival fallacy"—the false hope that "reaching some future destination will bring lasting happiness."[34] Once we get that new car, new promotion, or new location, however, that entity now belongs in our Box of Daily Experience, and we don't feel any different.

Lawrence shows how the triangle-headed character gets tricked into pursuing wanderlust, with the new sights and cultural experiences quickly dropping into the mundane order once again.[35]

Oh no! What the hell is this box doing here again?! How has it followed you all the way over here?!

---

34 Tal Ben-Shahar, *Happier: learn the secrets to daily joy and lasting fulfillment* (New York: McGraw-Hill, 2007).
35 Lawrence Yeo, "Travel Is No Cure for the Mind."

Perhaps it's time to find another place to go to?! Somewhere even further away?! A whole other continent maybe? Since The Box of Daily Experience has returned, the subsequent urge to break out of it has come back as well.

But here's the thing. Regardless of what you do to break out of the box, it won't work. You can change your external environment all you want, but you will continue to travel with the one box that will always accompany you.

The box known as your mind.

When I quit my job, I knew this was going to happen. I had seen it time and time again in my life, which is why I wasn't surprised when traveling to all these new places didn't cure me immediately. I've had profound travel experiences, energized by new people and new sights, and I've had others after which I felt more empty and lost than ever before, simply more tired and sick and significantly more broke than if I hadn't gone on the trip.

***

To me, this internal discomfort is remnant from what has become known as burnout. Difficult to separate from a constant low-grade anxiety or depression, burnout is what I came to know as an omnipresent listlessness, dissatisfaction, and exhaustion. Burnout is typically associated with the workplace. I wasn't simply tired of my job, however. It felt like I was burnt out from *life* itself.

The term "burnout" was coined in the 1970s by the American psychologist Herbert Freudenberger to describe effects of severe sacrifice and pressure appearing most commonly in those working in "helping" professions, such as doctors or nurses.[36] In current times, the term is used to encompass anyone who feels the consequences of chronic overwork and stress.

Lisa Freudenberger, daughter of the psychologist, described how her father worked with young drug addicts and watched them "literally holding cigarettes and watch the cigarettes burn out." When he pulled twelve hours on the Upper East Side and then went down to the Bowery to work until 2 a.m., he started to get more and more fatigued and stressed. He started becoming unpleasant to be around. His kids started staying out of his way. This escalated until he couldn't get out of bed to go on vacation with his family. As a therapist, Herbert conducted self-analysis and recorded his thoughts into a tape recorder: "I don't know how to have fun. I don't know how to be readily joyful."[37]

His mind thought of the drug addicts down on the Bowery with their blank looks and their cigarettes burning out, and he labeled his illness "burnout." As he described, "Burnout really is a response to stress. It's a response to frustration. It's a response to a demand that an individual may make upon themselves in terms of a requirement for perfectionism or drive."

---

36   Noel King, "When A Psychologist Succumbed To Stress, He Coined The Term 'Burnout'," December 8, 2016, in *Planet Money NPR*, podcast, 3:00.
37   Noel King, "When A Psychologist Succumbed To Stress, He Coined The Term 'Burnout'."

When Herbert came out with his hit book *Burnout: The High Cost Of High Achievement* in 1980, doctors and social workers and housewives alike sung out in a chorus of recognition. Since then, burnout has become a widely known issue, especially with Anne Helen Petersen's 2019 Buzzfeed article "How Millennials Became The Burnout Generation."[38] Exploring systemic issues such as student debt, the housing crisis, the performative nature of social media, and the race to optimization, Petersen writes that "[burnout] is not a temporary affliction: It's the millennial condition. It's our base temperature. It's our background music. It's the way things are. It's our lives."

Petersen expresses that her "own experience as a white, upper-middle-class, college-educated woman provided the backbone" of her original essay. Her follow-up article, "Here's What 'Millennial Burnout' Is Like For 16 Different People," includes more nuanced perspectives from people from marginalized backgrounds.[39] Some excerpts:

> *Elly: As a black woman I feel as if I were born tired. Every woman in my family has always worked since adolescence almost until the day they died. That's one thing I think is always missing from conversations about women in the workplace. To middle-class white women, work still seems like somewhat of a novelty. I'm an elementary school teacher. My mother was a social*

---

38 Anne Helen Petersen, "How Millennials Became The Burnout Generation," *Buzzfeed News*, January 5, 2019.

39 Anne Helen Petersen, "Here's What "Millennial Burnout" Is Like For 16 Different People," *Buzzfeed News*, January 9, 2019.

worker. My grandmother was a teacher and her mother was a slave. I was born burned out.

Clare: Hiding poverty is like hiding abuse at home—it's the reason you can't have friends over to your house, it's the reason you can't go to other kids' birthday and sleepover parties, it's the reason you can't go on the class trip, or summer camp, or vacations. But having to beg off, duck out, or provide a suitable explanation that good middle-class kids, parents, and teachers could even hear, that's hard. That's a lot of work for a kid. . . .

Hiding your poverty, performing middle-class-ness, and just plain not talking about class is something American culture seemingly requires of us as a baseline behavior, as a condition of survival, let alone advancement. It's what we poverty people do to get along, to keep real middle-class people from feeling uncomfortable or guilty. We devote so much energy and so much cognitive bandwidth to erasing whole swaths of the real conditions we live in so that we don't take up their bandwidth with uncomfortable feels or having to revise their assumptions or having to think about accommodating exceptions.

Daiyu: Mental health was not something we talked about in my household growing up. Depression and anxiety were not words I ever heard until my Psychology 100 class in my first year of undergrad. Instead, I heard the terms "eating bitterness" and "heart feeling" as both my parents felt the depression that is common for newcomers to Canada, struggling to find stable

> work in a society that places white folks above all others. Accepting the fact that I, too, can be burned out, depressed, and anxious while still being a Chinese person has been a tough process.
>
> Liz: Burnout, for me as a chronically ill and autistic person, is both where I live and what I spend most of my energy fighting via doctors and self-care. I am not able to work; my "job" is healthwork. I spend hours each day resting, taking care of my body and mind, and just trying to stay alive. It is never enough, because due to my conditions I am always in pain, always tired, always with less energy than I need to get through the tasks of the day.

I noticed the feelings of burnout often were hard to describe; people often used the term as an all-encompassing feeling, with "tired" as the most common additional descriptor. I decided to ask some of my own friends to describe what they explicitly mean when they experience burnout. Here are some of the replies:

> For me, burnout has been episodic and based on external circumstances like busy seasons at work/school, rather than an ongoing background feeling. I'll use college as an example: procrastinate all semester on my final projects/papers because of many factors (it's too hard, I want to avoid feeling stupid, I don't know how to break down these big tasks into smaller chunks, I don't know where to start, etc.) If I had to break it down:

- The week leading up to the due date rolls around and it's time to finally get started.
- Pull a few late nights or all-nighters and intensively devote my entire being to this one subject all week.
- Feel deeply overwhelmed and resentful of myself, school, and everyone in my life. Sleep deprivation exacerbates the shame spiral and makes me act like a monster to the people around me. Probably have at least one scream-crying meltdown.
- Turn in the assignment a day late because the meltdowns ate up valuable time, and then sleep for two days straight to catch up. Ignore any other responsibilities I might have because I'm sleeping.
- Still feel emotionally exhausted for weeks or months after the physical exhaustion is over. Question why I'm even doing this and if I want to keep going.
- Decide to finish college only because having student loans but no degree seems worse than finishing.

I'll bite off more than I can chew because I think that having a lot of responsibility is what makes me worthy of respect and admiration. But then, instead of taking consistent small actions toward those responsibilities, I'll get overwhelmed and procrastinate on them, which creates both indecision fatigue and puts me in the position to burn the candle at both ends when the deadline rolls around. Obviously, the bad habits with time management at the beginning are what create burnout in the long run, but I don't feel burnt out until that last week or so of intensive focus on the work I've been putting off.

I'm going through one of the "phases," or whatever you would like to call it, of burnout right now. The weird thing is I will typically feel like this for a few days, have a few great days, then hit the low again. I always get in a state of confusion and feel like I have lost passion for many things. I can't put my finger on the "trigger" and don't even know if there is a trigger. I think burnout can definitely feel very similar to a depressive state. Mine is tied very much to my business, and I let how I feel about my business in the short term determine how I feel about myself as a person and my worthiness in all areas of life.

My experience with burnout was particularly in regard to my teaching career. The part that I still find fascinating is that even while I was experiencing the burnout, I never once said that I didn't love my job. As a teacher, I felt this immense joy in being able to teach the kids and to be in the classroom, but I just didn't recognize that this was impacting so many other areas of my life. I probably felt a sense of shame in admitting that I wasn't happy as a teacher.

For me it looked like:

- Lethargy (I didn't want to do anything other than go to school, come home, eat, and go to bed).
- Retreating from social interactions with my family and friends. I suspect that this was linked to not having any energy, but I just continued to make excuses to not go to things unless I absolutely had to.

- Not exercising and eating stupid amounts of chocolate and comfort foods, which led to weight gain.
- Questioning myself and doubting every bit of positive feedback I was given.
- Eventually, this led to becoming so sick that I was forced to take three full weeks off school (at the worst possible time of the year). I was completed bedridden and it took me a very long time to recover!

This is such a complicated question to answer (seems too big to figure out where to start!) but I'll try:

It was a bit like not wanting to get up, being indifferent about everything, not even interested in things I enjoyed (which is why I stopped taking photos and playing my violin). I was clinically depressed, and it was a chicken and egg thing: I don't know if the burnout or depression came first but they were both definitely feeding off each other, along with the anxiety.

Everything felt hard: coming in to work on time, eating meals (I skipped a lot), and even taking showers. That season of my life was my lowest point and I'm so grateful to have gotten out of it.

I remember my former career coach advising me to stop stressing over not knowing what I wanted to do with my life because the burnout meant I wouldn't have that answer. I learned to just focus on my next right thing each day, which was to heal and rest and learn to reach out and enjoy life again.

According to Elizabeth Grace Saunders, a time management coach, a classic state of burnout makes people feel like everything is out of control, "as if everything around you is working against you."[40] In one comprehensive model of burnout developed by Christina Maslach, UC Berkeley professor and one of the foremost researchers on burnout, control is one of the six factors (the others being workload, reward, community, fairness, and values).[41] Burnout often appears in employees who have little autonomy over their day-to-day work.

For those who may think that burnout is all in your head—yes, it is. Burnout shows up quite literally in your head, causing physiological changes to the brain. In one study, those diagnosed with burnout reported more difficulty regulating their emotional responses to stressful stimuli of negative images and startling sounds.[42] In brain scans, participants with burnout and the control group showed key differences in the amygdala—a brain structure that is essential in controlling emotional responses, including fear, anger, aggression, and sadness. Those who reported stress also had weaker links between the amygdala and the anterior cingulate cortex (ACC) and the medial prefrontal cortex (mPFC), structures that control emotional distress and executive function, respectively. Individuals suffering from burnout respond

---

40 Elizabeth Grace Saunders, "To Recover from Burnout, Regain Your Sense of Control," *Harvard Business Review*, December 5, 2017.
41 Michael P. Leiter and Christina Maslach, "Six Areas of Worklife: A Model of the Organizational Context of Burnout," *Journal of Health and Human Services Administration* 21, no 4 (Spring 1999): 472-489.
42 Golkar, A et al., "The influence of work-related chronic stress on the regulation of emotion and on functional connectivity in the brain," *PLoS ONE* 9, no 9 (September 3, 2014): e104550.

with stronger emotions to seemingly smaller incidents or tasks.

Another study proved that chronic occupational stress is correlated with pronounced thinning of the frontal cortex, critical to cognitive functioning.[43] The brains of those experiencing burnout also showed significant reduction in gray matter volumes in the brain as well as memory, attention, and emotional difficulties, patterns similar to neuroimaging studies of people who have experienced severe early-life trauma.

I don't know if my frontal cortex has thinned or if the link between my amygdala and ACC is weaker, but I now know that I was most certainly experiencing burnout when I decided to walk out of my job.

***

A couple months after I embarked on my new journey, I realized that how I spent my free time before I quit my job was still how I spent my free time after. Beyond the beautiful places I visited, people I connected with, and projects I started, I didn't magically change—surprise! I still spent mornings scrolling and nights watching TV. The old thoughts were still there, with the physical tiredness still ingrained in my body. This time, I didn't even have my job to blame. Having consumed plenty of resources on this topic, I knew this was going to happen, and it did. Impatient to heal, I knew

---

[43] Savic, I., "Structural changes of the brain in relation to occupational stress," *Cerebral Cortex* 25, no. 6 (June 2015): 1554–1564.

I was the box in the Box of Daily Experience but was still annoyed with the box of myself.

To many, it seemed like I quit my job to travel the world. And to some extent, I did. Two days after I packed up my apartment, I took off on a road trip across the United States and wouldn't be in any given place for more than two weeks at a time for the next six months. I told myself that this time, the traveling wasn't for the new locations themselves. I didn't come to China to float on a bamboo raft or eat spices that lit my tongue on fire (though I did, and they were both beautiful experiences).

I came to play hide-and-seek with my niece and nephew, to learn mahjong from my aunt, and to take walks with my uncle and listen to him spout philosophy. I learn how to paint with a local artist three days in a row, to the point where she tells us stories about her husband and annoying habits about her daughter. I linger all afternoon at a teahouse, observing pedestrians and eavesdropping on conversations.

Trying to root myself in the present, I give my Box of Daily Experience a hug, getting a sliver of a taste of what wonder and joy feels like throughout my body. I try to hang on these moments as long as I can, sometimes to only feel them slipping away to settle into ingrained feelings of discomfort, numbing, and exhaustion.

PART 2

CHAPTER 6

EXACTLY WHERE I'M SUPPOSED TO BE

―

To be mindful (focusing on one thing at a time) and to meditate (focusing on one's mental processes) both involve no longer trying to satisfy one's thirst. Instead, we slow down and become more aware of that thirst, without evasion and without judgment.

—DAVID LOY

I'm sitting in a cafe in the middle of Manhattan, sipping on a $7 grainy matcha latte. It's the first time I've returned to the city since I tearily hugged my roommate goodbye and drove away in a car in the middle of the night with everything I owned. I haven't had a moment alone since I arrived until now, so I pull out my black leather notebook and begin to reflect.

The visit has been a whirlwind, packed with social appointments and social anxiety. Both are fueled from going months without having any social interaction outside of family. One friend plays hooky to accompany me to the Museum of Modern Art, where we twist our heads back and forth to look at optical illusions as confusing as our love lives. I visit the office, hugging previous coworkers and managers, chatting about my travels, and dodging questions about my future. "How are things?" I ask. "Oh, you know, same old same old," they say. I hear stories about others who have "pulled an Amy" (i.e., quit their job to take a break). I wonder what management thinks of this. I sit in parks and cafes and listen to hours of team dynamics and project issues. *Is there such a thing as an office therapist? I'd make a decent one,* I muse.

A friend and I brunch for almost four hours. We get our nails done, eat ice cream and watch movies, and whisper until 4 a.m. I meet another friend at a Halloween store for twenty minutes before parting ways. He rushes off to a film screening; I rush to a hot pot dinner. The friend I'm walking with answers work emails the entire way there, frustratingly pausing in the middle of the sidewalk to yell at her team. I discuss the classic love-hate relationship with the city and how to not numb feelings at my favorite Thai restaurant, the one with the ornate chandeliers. A friend and I hop through all the art galleries and shops in SoHo to escape the rain.

I put my pen down and take another sip from the mug. High schoolers trickle into the cafe and take all the seats next to me, pulling out homework and gossiping about what happened at the lockers. I look at the dotted pages, filled with people and activities and one single thought: *They're right, things are same old, same old. Except for me.* I notice myself letting go of any perceived judgment from others or myself, simply looking at the words as neutral events. I smile at the recognition that I'm changing and growing, thankful for the people who continue to support me for who I'm becoming.

Surrounded by backpacks and algebra textbooks and overpriced lattes, I have the overwhelming feeling that **I'm exactly where I'm supposed to be**. I hold my breath, as if I could hold onto this feeling as long as I don't exhale. I scribble on the page: *This is possible from within myself, not external circumstances.*

When the Buddha taught mindfulness, he always taught it as part of a whole. He never said, 'Pay attention to your breath and you will be free of suffering.' More like, 'Pay attention to your breath as a way of steadying the mind, and then look at your life.'

—CRAIG HASE AND DEVON HASE

Mindfulness. It's a word as commonplace as any other now. You'll find it on any clickbait list of "Seven secrets on how to be happy and successful," along with green tea, yoga, and reading.

I first got acquainted with the term in 2015. I had been practicing yoga off and on for years prior to that but hadn't done anything of the sort outside of it. The yoga classes I went to were at the YMCA and were the typical Westernization of physical, stretch yoga, filled with warrior poses and chaturangas. If there were acknowledgements of any mindfulness concepts, it was perhaps a reminder to breathe throughout the poses, or a mantra spoken at the end of class.

Our second year of college, my friend Penny and I decided to sign up for a mindfulness practice class together that met from 2-4 p.m. every Tuesday. UVA Engineering had sent the class information in an email to all first- and second-years, as faculty probably knew we should have mindfulness training to brace ourselves for the year ahead. I didn't have a real understanding of what it even was; I just knew it was related to meditation and that meditation was supposedly good for you. And I needed to do something that was good for me, especially for my mental and emotional state.

On our first day of class, our instructor, a middle-aged man with a beard and slow smile who told us to call him Sam, gathered us all in a circle to take turns saying what we thought mindfulness was. I had just started reading Eckhart Tolle's *The Power of Now: A Guide to Spiritual Enlightenment*, so when it came time for me to say something, I regurgitated a vague comment on mindfulness being the present moment, not really understanding what it meant.

So what exactly is mindfulness? We can't go through life without hearing mindful this, mindful that, but here's a quick definition just in case you haven't come across one that sticks with you yet.

Throughout the semester, the simplest definition that helped me truly understand the essence of mindfulness is that it is the act of *noticing,* or *awareness.* Jon Kabat-Zinn uses the following as a working definition: the awareness that emerges through paying attention on purpose, in the present moment, and nonjudgmentally to the unfolding of experience moment by moment.[44]

Mindfulness is not the present moment; it's the act of *noticing* that you're in the present moment. It's not the three breaths you take; it's the act of *observing* that you're taking each breath, one at a time. It's not clearing your mind, as people often misconstrue; it's the act of *realizing* you are having a thought. Mindfulness is that moment when you catch yourself. The practice of mindfulness is exactly that—a skill that you get better and better at with practice.

I looked forward to these two hours a week when I could practice this skill and be forced to simply sit and be still.

My electrical engineering lab ended at 1:50 p.m., so I had exactly ten minutes to run from the engineering school all the way to the nursing school where class was held. One week, Sam noticed me desperately drinking water to calm my frantic state from hustling up the stairs and pointed out the irony of hurrying to a mindfulness class. "Next time," he assured, "start your practice while on your walk to class and don't worry about being here exactly on time." I smiled in gratitude, wishing every professor could be as understanding as he was.

One of our first lessons in mindfulness is called the "body scan." We were taught a simple, twenty-minute exercise that

---

[44] John Kabat-Zinn, "Mindfulness-Based Interventions in Context: Past, Present, and Future." *Clinical Psychology Science and Practice* 10, no. 2 (June 2003): 144-156.

took us throughout each aspect of our body, starting from our toes and ending at the tops of our head. Meant for the breath to focus on something tangible, the body scan allowed us to be aware of the many parts of our body that we often take for granted.

The dozen or so of us all lay down on the carpeted floor, grabbing pillows and blankets to ensure we were as comfortable and relaxed as possible. Sam started the body scan. "Slowly bring your attention down to your feet. You might want to wiggle your toes a little. . . ." As he continued throughout the body, I suddenly noticed a soft, rhythmic noise coming from next to me, quickly growing more and more distracting.

Oh no, I thought to myself as I realized what was happening. *Someone is snoring.* I opened my eyes for only a second to sneak a peek to find out that the culprit was none other than Penny. I tried my best to dutifully continue the body scan but found myself caught in between secondhand embarrassment and holding myself back from laughing out loud.

I was no stranger to falling asleep during class myself. Given any opportunity to lay my head down, I could fall asleep in mere moments. My family would make fun of how I was the queen of cat naps. Any car ride, no matter if it was only ten minutes, was an opportunity to close my eyes and immediately fall asleep. However, I would always wake up right in time before getting to the destination. It was an uncanny sixth sense that I've had since I can remember.

Meditation classes showcased my ability to fall asleep almost instantly if given the opportunity to close my eyes and relax.

This ability was probably also a result of the sleep deprivation I experienced in college. I always woke up right as we were coming out of it, never missing the final moments and the ding of the bell that signified the end of any session.

I participated in a six-day, mostly silent, meditation retreat the next spring. The following is an excerpt from my journal:

March 5, 2016 at 9:16 a.m., Serenity Ridge Retreat Center in Shipman, Virginia

Today begins my first full day of the mindfulness retreat. My intention today is to stay awake during meditation and not fall asleep.

~1:30 p.m.

I did not fulfill that intention very well ^

Even though every instructor has said, "There is no being bad or good at mindfulness; it's a non-striving practice," I thought I was *terrible* at meditating. If my mind wasn't going everywhere, mulling over to-do lists or past conversations or what I was going to eat for dinner, I was falling asleep. However, slowly but surely, I began to train my mind and catch myself more and more. Instead of going down a rabbit hole of ten different thoughts, I caught myself thinking after two or three thoughts instead, reminding myself, "Wait, I'm thinking. Let me focus on the breath again."

Being gentle and reminding ourselves that there is no "good" or "bad" performance in mindfulness allows us to show up each and every time without expectations. I might have thought I was terrible, but accepting myself as I was allowed me to be kinder to myself, and in turn, make space for the growth I was seeking.

When someone tells me that they're just "not a meditation person," I don't buy it. *No, I want to tell them, you're just bad at it.* My mind leaps into judgment mode, making connections to how a complete beginner who starts classical piano or rock climbing isn't going to be a "piano person" or a "rock climbing person" immediately because it's uncomfortable. But I don't say any of that. The whole point of mindfulness is that there is no "good" or "bad"; it just is. It's the strangest contradiction, and one that took me consistent practice to embrace. The acceptance of what is, releasing any sort of judgment or resistance, allows growth in peace and clarity.

Between stimulus and response there is a space. In that space is our power to choose our response. In our response lies our growth and our freedom.

—VICTOR FRANKL

Sure, meditation is helpful during those minutes when we sit down to breathe. The real practice, however, comes later on. Can we cultivate that awareness when our bodies are trying to tell us something? Or when a family member triggers an emotional reaction? Are we able to catch ourselves, over and over again, when we're not listening to a guide reminding us to return to the breath?

Before Thanksgiving break, Sam took a survey of the room to ask who felt stressed when going back home. Every single person in the room raised their hand or nodded in agreement. Since most of us were returning to environments we had very little control over, he encouraged us to think of the time as lessons in mindfulness, especially to practice patience. Knowing that each trigger from family members served as an opportunity to exercise mindfulness and patience reframed everything for me. Instead of instinctively being annoyed, I could be thankful that I had the opportunity to execute what I had learned. I've carried that lesson ever since Sam described it to us. Every time I encounter a feeling of irritation, from family or otherwise, I try my best to remember that it is an opportunity to break out of my habit and respond with grace and understanding.

One class, Sam had us all sit down in a circle to listen to him read a chapter from Jonathan Haidt's *The Happiness Hypothesis: Finding Modern Truth in Ancient Wisdom*. The first chapter titled "The Divided Self" outlines a central metaphor for the mind Haidt has personally used for over ten years—a rider and an elephant.[45] Using examples of Freud, Plato, Buddha, and the Roman poet Ovid to depict how "desire and reason are pulling in different directions," Haidt describes how most of the time, he succumbs to the powerlessness of doing things he knows are bad for him. We all came up with our own examples: ignoring our alarm clocks even though we know we have to get up, refusing to go on a run even though we told ourselves we were serious about

---

45 Haidt, Jonathan, *The Happiness Hypothesis: Finding Modern Truth in Ancient Wisdom* (New York: Basic Books, 2006), 1-6.

working out this time, or telling ourselves *just one more episode* before going to bed.

We sat with our meditation cushions beneath us, listening to Haidt's words:

> *The image that I came up with for myself, as I marveled at my weakness, was that I was a rider on the back of an elephant. I'm holding the reins in my hands, and by pulling one way or the other I can tell the elephant to turn, to stop, or to go. I can direct things, but only when the elephant doesn't have desires of his own. When the elephant really wants to do something, I'm no match for him.*

The elephant and rider metaphor stems from Buddha's words: "Today this mind does not stray and is under the harmony of control, even as a wild elephant is controlled by the trainer."

There are many other names for this concept. I grew up in the Christian church, learning the vocabulary for this as "the flesh." In the Bible, Galatians 5:16–18 tells us: "But I say, walk by the Spirit, and you will not gratify the desires of the flesh. For the desires of the flesh are against the Spirit, and the desires of the Spirit are against the flesh, for these are opposed to each other, to keep you from doing the things you want to do."

Another name besides the elephant or the flesh is the monkey mind, a term originating in Buddhism. Tim Urban, one of the Internet's most beloved writers with his blog *Wait But*

Why, popularized the monkey mind with his 2013 article "Why Procrastinators Procrastinate."[46] In Urban's stick figure drawings, he has two figures in the brain: Rational Decision-Maker saying, "I do things that make sense. I think long-term. I am not a child," and a little creature called Instant Gratification Monkey, saying, "Nope!"

Whenever Rational Decision-Maker wants to do anything remotely useful or good, Instant Gratification Monkey always has other plans. These plans include a bunch of videos on deep sea creatures, a series of Richard Feynman talks on string theory, and interviews with Justin Bieber's mom. Monkey has it all figured out. Eat when you're hungry, drink when you're thirsty, sleep when you're tired, and don't do anything difficult. Rational Decision-Maker doesn't know how to fight against Instant Gratification Monkey.

Just as we have to train our monkey minds, the rider has to be ready to pull the reins to respond to the elephant's desire. Practicing mindfulness is one way to strengthen the rider so that the rider is able to nudge the elephant in the right direction.

I'm reminded of when I told myself I wasn't the plastic pony and instead the rider. In that moment, I remembered that I had trained the rider to be in control of decisions.

---

46   Urban, Tim. "Why Procrastinators Procastinate." *Wait But Why*, October 30, 2013.

Mindfulness is not the cure. Rather, mindfulness sets the foundation, allowing the space for discerning what the next right step is. Through cultivating awareness, we can listen to the space between stimulus and response and choose action with clarity, not reactivity.

CHAPTER 7

FREE YOUR FEELINGS

We are a culture of people who've bought into the idea that if we stay busy enough, the truth of our lives won't catch up with us.

–BRENÉ BROWN

Staring outside the car window looking at endless farmland, the thought *I have nothing to do* keeps repeating in my head. This thought is different than the "nothing to do" time when you finish exams and go party or spend a week in bed recovering watching TV. Or when a three-day weekend creeps up and you didn't even realize it so you have nothing to do except push back the Sunday Scaries a day later. This "nothing to do" is unlike anything I had experienced before. For the first time in my entire life, there's no deadline, no start date, no deliverable, no to-do list. My calendar is as blank as the wide, rolling plains of Iowa passing by.

It's terrifying.

A week later, I toss and turn underneath the star-filled skies of Wyoming with nothing to distract me, not even cell service. Boredom and restlessness hum through my veins, bringing up thoughts I had forgotten to the surface. My entire body feels everything at once.

Oh no. My life is catching up to me.

* * *

When I took the Myers-Briggs Type Indicator personality test for the first time in seventh grade, I tried to answer against my feelings as much as possible. *I'm calculated. I'm smart. I'm logical,* I told the test. No wonder I placed myself in an Introverted, Intuitive, Thinking, and Judging (INTJ) box. It matched the projected image of my Capricorn nature very well.

The same year, my piano teacher told my parents, "Amy is a very sensitive girl." This was most likely due to the simultaneous tears and stubbornness she witnessed week after week on the piano bench. I remember my mom telling me my sensitivity was a gift, as if it were a good thing—something to embrace. *Sensitive??* Rage bubbled up. I couldn't see the irony of my anger.

I took the Myers-Briggs test again in college. *INFJ,* it told me—Introverted, Intuitive, Feeling, and Judging. Somehow, along the way, I allowed myself to feel, with even a (meaningless) test score to prove it.

108 · RECLAIMING CONTROL

One class that taught me how to feel was called a "Buddhist Approach to Development." For our final exam, we had to write one page on what grade we thought we deserved and three pages on the lessons we would take with us moving forward. The first paragraph of my takeaways is as follows:

> Much of what I learned in this class is difficult to put into words. Thinking to what was most impactful from this class, most of my memories are feelings. The connection I felt when we read our anonymous journals or shared our final projects. The peace that permeated throughout my body while meditating in the garden. The sense of curiosity for anything and everything around me when I pressed my feet in the damp grass in the midst of birds and trees. The pure contentment after each class period on Monday and Wednesday evenings. The emptiness when dwelling on the concept of no-self too much. The confusion from reading about how to be human. The aha moments of realization that everything is connected.

Feelings. What I wanted to remember were those feelings of connection, peace, curiosity, contentment, emptiness, confusion, and realization.

Without realizing it, I slipped back into numbing my feelings when I started working full time. During this time, at least nine hours from Monday to Friday were dedicated to professional suppressing. Evenings and weekends consisted of more social activities that required a mask of happiness. Most days, I was simply too tired to feel anything and too scared to even approach the subject. If I had space to myself, I continued to numb myself with Netflix or sleep.

When we think about numbing with external entities, we often think about substances such as drugs or alcohol. While those are still serious issues, we can use anything as a distraction to take the edge off. From infinite scrolling to video games to refreshing news feeds, short-term dopamine hits are always available at our fingertips.

Brené Brown writes about addiction in her book *The Gifts of Imperfection: Let Go of Who You Think You're Supposed to Be and Embrace Who You Are*:[47]

> For me, it wasn't just the dance halls, cold beer, and Marlboro Lights of my youth that got out of hand—it was banana bread, chips and queso, e-mail, work, staying busy, incessant worrying, planning, perfectionism, and anything else that could dull those agonizing and anxiety-fueled feelings of vulnerability.

Fueled by constant stimulation and instant gratification, we rarely give ourselves the space to understand our emotions. Dr. Marc Brackett, founding director of Yale Center for Emotional Intelligence, introduces this issue in his book *Permission to Feel: Unlocking the Power of Emotions to Help Our Kids, Ourselves, and Our Society Thrive*:[48]

---

47 Brené Brown, *The Gifts of Imperfection: Let Go of Who You Think You're Supposed to Be and Embrace Who You Are* (Minnesota: Hazelden Publishing, 2010).

48 Marc Brackett, *Permission to Feel: Unlocking the Power of Emotions to Help Our Kids, Ourselves, and Our Society Thrive* (Celadon Books, 2019).

Do I even know how I'm feeling? Have I given myself permission to ask? Have I ever really asked my partner, my child, my colleague? Today, when nearly every question can be handled instantly by Siri, or Google, or Alexa, we're losing the habit of pausing to look inward, or to another, for answers. . . . Google can't tell you why your son or daughter is feeling hopeless or excited, or why your significant other feels not so significant lately, or why you can't shake that chronic low-level anxiety that plagues you.

When I created space in my life, much of the "chronic low-level anxiety" became intermittent high-level anxiety. I wasn't always "fine" anymore. I felt more alive, with both the good and the bad, and more in tune with the sensations in my body. I learned how to listen to what my body was telling me and to sit with the emotions that were finally allowed to surface.

I spoke about mind-body awareness with Dr. Dara Blumenthal, who is trained as a sociologist, developmental coach, and integral facilitator. Dara explained how she takes people out of the abstract narrative of what people think emotions are, leading them deeper into the sensation of emotion itself. She told me, "If you're going to deal with discomfort, you're going to have to come out of the abstract and be where you are right now. You're going to start to feel things you're avoiding all the time." Working with mindfulness-based somatic psychotherapy, she guides people into the felt experience of the present moment. "So often, people will continually *think* about how they're feeling. We don't think to actually stop and *feel* what we're feeling."

As humans, we experience emotions across the entire range of possibilities. Over time, we've been conditioned to accept a dichotomy of negative and positive emotions. Feelings such as happiness, gratitude, courage, and contentment are labeled as good. Feelings such as envy, greed, sadness, and anger are labeled as bad. When these negative feelings arise, most people try to distance themselves immediately, getting caught in a spiral of avoidance and shame. Dara trains people to stay with their felt experience instead of distancing from discomfort.

Dara's work makes me think of a well-known Buddhist parable about two arrows. As meditation teacher and author Tara Brach explains, the first arrow is the natural experience that arises, for example: fear, aggression, greed, craving. The second arrow is self-aversion to the fact of the first arrow.[49] We don't like ourselves for having experiences of being nasty, selfish, or greedy. The Buddha says, "The first arrow hurts; why do we shoot the second arrow into us, ourselves?" And yet we do. He goes on to say, "In life, we cannot always control the first arrow; however, the second arrow is our reaction to the first. The second arrow is optional." The human condition, the first arrow, comes from circumstances beyond our control. When we train ourselves to release the judgment and blame we experience in response to the first arrow, the second arrow becomes completely avoidable.

In our conversation, Dara reminded me that mindfulness is a tool—a powerful tool, but neutral in its own right. She

---

49   Tara Brach, "The Wisdom of 'It's Not My Fault': Finding Freedom When We are Caught in Self-Blame," *Tara Brach*, August 9, 2017.

laughed, saying, "Anyone can be super mindful and a terrible person. You can be really mindful and destroy the earth. It's not enough to just be mindful. It's really vital to become mindful of what your experiences are to start to locate where you want to be operating from." To Dara, that operating space is emotional development, because it's working in an interpersonal dynamic with yourself and others.

In order to manage thoughts and subsequently feelings, it is firstly most important to be able to understand both thoughts and emotions with compassion and curiosity, without judgment, shame, or any semblance of beating yourself up. Mindfulness practice is important because in order to understand emotions, we must first be able to feel them in the body. Then comes the recognition of the story we are telling ourselves around that emotion, which stems from our thoughts.

If we are able to sit with that awareness around the sensations and thoughts, we can then understand the patterns without trying to immediately change them. By accepting they are present, we can then give the space to understand with true compassion. Without judging ourselves, we are able to wonder, "Is this how I want to feel?" and if not, follow up with, "How do we want to feel?" and, "What can we think or do to feel this way?"

I'm responsible for my own happiness? I can't even be responsible for my own breakfast!
–BOJACK HORSEMAN

Danielle Laporte, best-selling author, entrepreneur, and inspirational speaker, has centered her life's work on the concept of desired feelings.[50] This revelation came to her one New Year's Eve, when she decided to have a chill evening at home to reflect and plan, complete with the fireplace crackling and lots of Ruffles chips and ranch dip. Along with her former husband, she found some poster board and divided it into various life sections, including work, home, love, and money. They'd write a goal, sneak in a smooch, grab some chips, rinse, and repeat.

New kitchen table. Pay off credit card. Lose ten pounds. Start biking to work. Publishing deal. Find a yoga class. The list went on and on. Danielle stared at the board, feeling like something was amiss. It felt eager, but not fully alive. The goals didn't match the inspired ambition she was feeling within her heart. Not realizing exactly what she was doing, she pulled out a different colored pen and started scrawling feeling words in each section.

Abundance. True love. Freedom! Creative. Connected.

She turned to her husband and asked, "How do you want to feel at work?"

He answered, "Courageous. Confident. Adventurous."

That question turned the planning and the goal-setting itself inside out, and they started the process all over. This time,

---

50 Danielle Laporte, *The Desire Map: A Guide to Creating Goals with Soul* (Sounds True, 2014).

the exercises felt more energizing. Their list of wants also started to morph into something more heart-centered.

Have a dinner party once a month. Design a line of thank-you cards. Two-week canoe trip. Self-publish.

Danielle writes that the board visually started to look more beautiful, and within themselves, it felt like an "invitation rather than another list of things to do."

On several more New Year's Eves, they wrote on their "feelings 'n' goals thing," noticing that they didn't feel so disappointed when they didn't check off *Lose ten pounds* or *Paris*, because it wasn't about the goal itself. Danielle could see that her two trips to New York and the new yoga classes fulfilled those desired states of being that the weight and travel goals were targeting. There was progress because she was feeling the way she wanted to feel, being compassionate to herself. Ironically, this gentler, more fluid approach didn't let her off the hook. It was actually motivating her to align her desires with her core values. It became more transparent when she wasn't feeling very free or creative due to certain actions she was taking. She gave the "feelings 'n' goals thing" a name, the Strategy of Desire, and started a movement around knowing how you want to feel and how to generate those feelings.

As Danielle summarizes, "You're not chasing the goal, you're chasing a feeling you hope reaching the goal will give you."

I got to try the process out for myself when a friend wanted a life makeover after having gotten out of a long-term relationship. Since my new apartment didn't have a couch yet, the two of us sat on the floor of my living room, flipping through Danielle's *The Desire Map: A Guide to Creating Goals with Soul* exercises together. Munching on chips and salsa, we went through a series of rapid-fire questions from the book.

The color of joy? Sparkling yellow, rainbow, sunrise.

The sound of joy? A baby's laughter, the clinks of wine glasses, splashes in the swimming pool.

The scent of joy? Chocolate chip cookies, coffee in the morning, slightly burnt marshmallows.

With each question, I could see my friend smile despite heartbreak as she thought of what joy meant to her. Perhaps the process did work.

Curious as to how other people found the gap between current and desired emotions, I texted a few friends the question, "Day to day, what are the top three emotions you feel?" Some of the answers are as follows:

Grateful. Relieved. Determined.
Love. Boredom. Nostalgia.
On a good day: Curiosity. Inspiration. Excitement. On a bad day: Apathy. Anxiety-induced procrastination. Loneliness.
uhhh. hard to say. idk... Self-remorse. Relief. Nostalgia Homesickness. Thankfulness. Worry.

I followed up with the question, "How do you *want* to feel day to day?" In no respective order to the above, these are some of the responses:

> *Huh. I've never really thought about that. I guess happy? Inspired. Productive.*
> *Connected. Energized. Content.*
> *Love. Peace. Joy.*
> *Anything but stagnant.*
> *Organized. Focused. True to self.*

Out of all the answers I got, only one feeling with one person made it on both their current and desired states.

How do we work to close this gap? For me, I found that answer with the questions "What if we acted as if there were no gap in the first place? What if we were already at our desired states?"

Love sometimes wants to do us a great favor: hold us upside down and shake all the nonsense out.
Ever since happiness heard your name, it has been running through the streets trying to find you.
I wish I could show you when you are lonely or in the darkness, the astonishing light of your own being.

–HAFEZ

When I was in Costa Rica, I started reading *There Will be No Miracles Here,* a memoir by Casey Gerald. Almost every night after a full day of class, I'd pull out the book from the drawer underneath my bunk bed, wipe off the musty pages from the humidity from rainy season, and read on the hammock with my flashlight outside of the bamboo bunkhouse.

On paper, Casey Gerald is a rags-to-riches, American Dream poster child: growing up near-orphaned in small-town Texas, attending Yale University on a football scholarship and attending Harvard for his MBA, working in finance, founding a nonprofit that empowers entrepreneurs across the United States, and going viral for his TED Talk "The Gospel of Doubt," all before the age of thirty.[51]

He was prescribed a path to success just like so many of us are—do *x*, *y*, and *z* to become a certain person, and then you will be handed success. We've been told this narrative for our entire lives. In his words, "The cost of that prescription is ourselves," and the way we're taught to live is literally killing us.

When Casey was three months into writing his book, one of his closest friends from college committed suicide, one whom he had helped recruit to Yale. One night, after being heartbroken and not being able to write for days, Casey went to sleep, and his friend came to him in a dream. Sitting at a booth in a diner, he leaned back and said, "You know Casey, we did a lot of things that we wouldn't advise anybody we love to do."[52]

---

51 Casey Gerald, *There Will Be No Miracles Here: A Memoir* (New York: Penguin Publishing Group, 2018).
52 Brittany Luse and Eric Eddings, "You Don't Make Free People," August 15, 2009, in the *Nod*. podcast, 52:00.

At that point, Casey turned his memoir into a confession. A confession of how he drove his friend, and the others around him, to be perfect, and "to make people aware of how to divest ourselves from the belief that our worth, basic human value, is tied to institutions and spaces which were not designed for us to be free or to thrive."

After reading the book, I didn't really think much more of Casey Gerald until three months later, when I listened to his episode on the *Nod* podcast titled "You Don't Make Free People."[53]

One of the critiques to Casey Gerald's book is that he doesn't give answers. When talking about this on the *Nod*, he laughs and says that he didn't give answers that readers wanted to hear. One answer Casey sticks to now is meditation, so that he can constantly be in touch with his feelings. Understanding that personal freedom and success is "much more primal than it is philosophical." He states that "you don't make free people—you recover your freedom that was already there."

I stopped when I heard the line, "You don't make free people. You recover your freedom that was already there."

This concept was a key takeaway from when I participated in a silent meditation retreat. One instructor told us the Rumi quote, "Your task is not to seek for love, but merely to seek and find all the barriers within yourself that you have built against it." I scribbled down the quote in my journal, putting brackets around [love] and [you] so it reads as the following:

---

53   Brittany Luse and Eric Eddings, "You Don't Make Free People."

Your task is not to seek for [love], but merely to seek and find all the barriers within yourself that [you] have built against it.

At the time, I put brackets around "love" because I realized that within the brackets, you could insert whatever feeling you wanted: courage, joy, fulfillment—or in Casey's case, freedom. The brackets around "you" signify not only barriers that your own mind has constructed, but most of all what you have absorbed—from family, society, greater structures beyond ourselves—that end up as part of "you."

I continued listening to what Casey had to say, amazed at the connections I was making in my own life. With one of his tenets being meditation, he's come to understand what it means to already be free and do the work to break down the barriers that have obstructed that freedom.

Doing the work. Partly popularized by the likes of Byron Katie,[54] we hear that term all the time when it comes to the difficult, inner, messy life stuff. What does doing the work actually look like in practice? To Gerald, it was his meditation practice, coupled with his therapy practice of being able to feel negative feelings.[55]

It was being able to sit with his sadness, to sit and weep and not fight the tears but instead let them come. It was learning how to reframe mental health issues. When discussing anxiety, he said, "I deal with anxiety. Which is very different from saying, which I used to say and I know a lot

---

54 Katie Byron, "The Work is a Practice," *The Work of Byron Katie*, updated 2020.
55 Brittany Luse and Eric Eddings, "You Don't Make Free People."

of people will say, 'I have anxiety.' You don't have nothing. You deal with anxiety. Somebody will call me and say, 'Oh, my anxiety sure is bothering me today,' and I say, 'When did it become yours?'"

Most of all, when discussing inner freedom, Casey highlights how his ancestors have so much to teach when it comes to unlearning the slave mentality.

When talking about how his people survived being slaves, Casey points to a piece of art made by Ja'Tovia Gary, an artist and filmmaker based in Brooklyn, bringing together footage of Ruby Dee telling the story of a woman, Miss Fannie Moore, who was interviewed by the Federal Writers' Project about her mother who had been a slave.

One day she's in the field and gets all happy and starts shouting, and the master comes down and says, "What's all this hootin' and hollerin' for? I sent you out here to work. You better work or I'll put this cowhide against your Black back."

And her mother says, "The Lord has showed me the way and we ain't gonna be, never gonna be slaves no more. I don't care how you all treat me and my children. We, we are not gonna be slaves anymore." So then he starts whipping her. And as he's whipping her, Fannie Moore's mother starts shouting, saying, "I'm free. I'm free."

Casey explains how sometimes all he says is the same thing that Fanny Moore's mother said: "I'm free." He wakes up in the morning and walks through the day, repeating, "I'm free. I'm free. I'm free," even if he feels miserable. He asks himself, "Well, if that were true, how would I behave? If I am free, would I be so freaked out that I'm gonna be five minutes late? Would I entertain this thought that me being late is gonna ruin my career?" Laughing, Casey continues to entertain the thought of how being free would manifest in his life: "If I were actually free, would I do that thing I know I don't want to do? Would I say yes to that thing that I know is going to deplete me?"

The more he asks himself that, and the more he tries, the more he fails but doesn't give up. The freedom shows up in a truer and realer way. He says it all comes down to showing up and "doing the work," and that "the price is enormous, but it's a beautiful, beautiful, beautiful adventure."

A beautiful adventure. I understand that I will never understand the undeniable trauma that occurs from both past and present horrific racial injustice toward Black people. I can, however, embark on my own beautiful adventure and understand and unlearn what my ancestors and I have learned throughout time.

If I were truly embodying desired states of love, freedom, and courage, I wouldn't be doing things that opposed those values. I wouldn't be scared of feeling everything at once, because that's what it means to be human. I'd show up for myself in those ways, knowing I am already full of love, freedom, and courage.

Each moment is an opportunity to think, do, and feel based on whatever state we want. We can choose to act according to existing barriers, or we can remove them, knowing we already have full permission to show up as who we desire to be. Over time, these moments add up, creating how we define our lives.

CHAPTER 8

THE UNLOCKED CAGE

Most of us have two lives. The life we live, and the unlived life within us. Between the two stands Resistance.
–STEVEN PRESSFIELD

This is my life now. This is my life now. This is my life now.

I fill the page with these words as I sit on a slab of rock, looking out at a lake in the middle of Wyoming.

I had lived most of my life in preparation for something. In middle school, I was preparing for high school. In high school, I was preparing for college. In college, I was preparing to get a job. After graduating, I turned to what I saw everyone else preparing for, including promotions, next jobs, or graduate school. There's always a next step.

At first, I wonder what it would be like to press pause for a little bit. Just to catch my breath. What I realize, however, is that I don't simply want to press pause. I want to live in the present, not as a ghost daydreaming about the future or hung up on the past. I want to allow myself to dream, and then live those dreams in real time.

My shoulders tense and my stomach knots as I think about actually living life and questioning what I want.

I don't know what I want. I'm too indecisive to live my own life.

Feelings of self-doubt and overwhelm cloud my mind for a bit until I get annoyed. I say, "I don't know," to almost everything; I'm even sick of it myself. It's the same feeling when I'm at a restaurant staring at a huge menu, and the server has already come around three times to ask what I'd like to order. "Just a little more time, please," I always sheepishly respond.

I toss a pebble into the lake, watching it create ripples upon ripples. Impatience bubbles up inside me, letting me know that my time is up.

This is my life now.

***

Sitting at my desk one night, paralyzed by fear, I think, *No wonder people blindly go through the motions of life. This actual living life thing is scary.*

This fear permeates all of my thoughts. *What will people think of me? I don't even know what to think of me. Am I being completely irresponsible? Do my parents think I'm a failure? Are my friends as supportive as they seem, or do they think I've gone off the deep end?*

I faintly hear my mom teaching art to a student downstairs. "What do you want to draw next week? Let's pick something out together." She poses the question as her seven-year-old student colors finishing touches on the glossy, gold-tipped dragon wings.

"Godzilla!" He shouts immediately.

"Godzilla?" My mom responds, "Are you sure you want to draw something so scary?"

"Sometimes scary is beautiful, too," he states matter-of-factly, then names other monsters he wanted to bring to life.

Sometimes scary is beautiful, too.

I continue to sit with my monsters for a bit, naming them just like the seven-year-old boy downstairs. Perhaps I too will find them beautiful one day.

To do so, I need to stop avoiding them and learn to face them head on.

I will not be like a bird bred in a cage, too dull to fly even when the door stands open.
–MADELINE MILLER, CIRCE

When my friend Beza couldn't access consistent professional counseling for chronic anxiety and OCD, she turned to the Internet for answers. She came across exposure therapy, which "is intended to help the patient face and gain control of the fear and distress that was overwhelming in the trauma."[56] Determined to take matters into her own hands, she told herself she had nothing to lose. When the anxiety told her she couldn't step outside her dorm, she forced herself to walk outside and go to class. Though terrified of being alone, she started going to dining halls and grabbing coffee on her own. When she was able to talk herself through facing her fears, her body was able to see that there wasn't a true threat. She was able to start living her life again by exposing herself to the very situations she was so afraid of. "Anxiety makes you feel so out of control and makes you think that there's really nothing you can do to get better," Beza said. "I had to be the bigger voice. I had to get better."

When Beza told me her story, I was reminded of the notable series of learned helplessness experiments dating back to 1967, conducted by Steven Maier and Martin Seligman.[57] They repeatedly administered painful shocks to dogs that were trapped in locked cages, triggering a condition called "inescapable shock." After the cages were opened, the dogs that had been previously shocked did not run away. They simply lay there, whimpering. The only way to teach the traumatized dogs to get off the electric grids when the doors were open was to *repeatedly drag them out of their cages* so they could physically experience *how* they could get away.

---

56 John M. Grohol, "What is Exposure Therapy?" *PsychCentral*, October 8, 2018.
57 Martin E. Seligman and Steven F. Maier, "Failure to escape traumatic shock," *Journal of Experimental Psychology* 74, 1 (1967): 1-9.

Maier and Seligman have since proven that the "learned" part of this helplessness is not actually learned; it's simply the default mammalian response to prolonged bad events.[58] They emphasize what *can* be changed and that "this passivity can be overcome by learning control." Beza was able to rise above her default helplessness and learn to actively take control over her mind and body. Over time, this became a learned muscle that she was able to call on more on more when necessary.

This series of experiments plays a notable role in Dr. Bessel van der Kolk's book, *The Body Keeps the Score: Brain, Mind, and Body in the Healing of Trauma*. This book shows how trauma is universal, going beyond what people typically think of how extreme acute trauma is defined. Smaller, prolonged instances can have physical, mental, and emotional impacts similar to strong, acute events.[59]

Dr. Van der Kolk presents how trauma lives in the cells of our physical body, even when our mind may have put thoughts or memories of such trauma aside. Providing a sense of leadership over the body is critical for training our physical cells that danger is not immediate. Through active rebuilding of a sense of mind-body ownership, "taking effective action reinstates a sense that your organism is not a helpless tool of fate."[60]

---

58 Steven F. Maier and Martin E. P. Seligman. "Learned Helplessness at Fifty: Insights forom Neuroscience." *Psychol Rev.* 123, no. 4 (July 2016): 349-367.
59 Bessel van der Kolk, *The Body Keeps the Score: Brain, Mind, and Body in the Healing of Trauma* (New York: Penguin Books, 2015).
60 Bessel van der Kolk and Ruth Buczynski, "Four Concrete Steps for Working with Trauma," *New York Association of Psychiatric Rehabilitation*, November 18, 2015.

When I was burnt out, my entire being felt as if it had lost the ability to feel anything other than discomfort and exhaustion. The awareness didn't help anything; it was simply the foundation of what I had to do next. To learn how to feel better again, I had to repeatedly drag myself out of habitual thought patterns. I had to force myself to do things I knew to be fun. I never wanted to watch sunsets or go to the beach or play badminton, things I knew I loved, but I followed through anyway. Like the dogs in the cages, the door was fully open, but I (and sometimes my friends or my parents) still had to physically drag myself out.

The door is always fully open; it's never locked. In Glennon Doyle's memoir *Untamed*, she writes about her friend Ashley who goes to a hot yoga class for the first time.[61] Entering the class, the instructor announces, "You are going to get very hot, but you can't leave this room. No matter how you begin to feel, stay strong. Don't leave." After a few minutes, Ashley begins to feel sick and light-headed. She blacks out briefly, twice. All she wants to do is run toward the door, but she is terrified of breaking the instructor's rules. Holding back tears, she spends ninety minutes terrified and close to hyperventilating.

Once the class is up, Ashley jumps off her mat and runs into the bathroom. Flinging the door open, she vomits all over the bathroom floor. Wiping her own puke with paper towels on her hands and knees, she thinks, *What is wrong with me? Why did I stay and suffer? The door wasn't even locked.*

---

61   Glennon Doyle, *Untamed* (New York: Random House Publishing Group, 2020), 38.

Reading about Ashley wiping up her vomit from the floor gave me flashbacks of me scrubbing my own blood from the shower floor. In that case, there wasn't even an instructor telling me I couldn't leave the room. I simply accepted the default state of my helplessness until my body gave way. Like Ashley, my body gave me signals that I heard and ignored. I hadn't yet learned how to take action on my own.

The way through the challenge is to get still and ask yourself, 'What is the next right move? What is the next right move?' and then, from that space, make the next right move and the next right move.

—OPRAH WINFREY

Spoiler alert In the hit Disney movie *Frozen II*, there comes a point when Anna is left alone without the support of her loved ones. She has no idea where her sister Elsa is and only knows that she's far, far away and most likely not alive anymore. Her best friend, Olaf, flurries away in Anna's arms as the magic fades away. Completely alone, Anna hunches over in tears, numb with grief. She stays down for a bit, wallowing in despair. As she's crying, however, she hears a tiny voice whispering that she must go on and "do the right next thing." Lost and directionless, she doesn't know how to rise without any external guide or the previous compass of her sister. The whispering voice continues, telling her that taking one step is enough. Anna rises from the cold, hard ground and simply takes one step. Unable to look too far ahead, she breaks down each move and focuses on her next breath. Finding the courage to take one step at time, her steps quicken, allowing her to leap into action as she realizes what she has to do to save her kingdom.[62]

When Kristen Bell, the voice of Anna, discusses this scene, she says she sourced from her own struggles to give her character autonomy. Kristen admits, "I'm ferociously co-dependent, and it's taken me a long time to learn what to do when I'm alone." Recognizing Anna's relationship with the individuals around her, including Elsa, Kristoff, and Olaf, she told screenwriter and director Jennifer Lee that she "would really like to see Anna face her codependency head-on."[63]

Kristen has become quite outspoken about her journey with depression and anxiety, though she still gets uncomfortable every time she talks about it. "I feel this little tiny feeling bubble inside my belly that's like, 'Don't talk about that stuff.' It's in my bones, because we as a society want to put our best foot forward," she says. Drawing on Anna's song about simply taking the next step, she concludes, "I just, I don't believe in that. I just think I've become a person that's a firm believer in 'whatever foot goes forward.'"[64]

When we're left seemingly entirely alone without a North Star to guide us, it's up to us to develop that internal compass. It's difficult to know what the "right" step forward is, so sometimes we simply need to take whatever step moves

---

62   *Frozen II*, directed by Jennifer Lee and Chris Buck (2019; Burbank, CA: Walt Disney Pictures), film.
63   Lulu Garcia-Navarro and Emma Bowman, "For 'Frozen II,' Kristen Bell Found Inspiration In Personal Pain," *NPR*, December 8, 2019.
64   Ibid.

us in a direction, *any* direction. After that first move, we are able to assess and recalibrate as necessary.

Depression taught me how to break down action into the babiest of steps. In the midst of some of my most depressive states, I had to coax myself to do something—anything. Getting out of bed was a nearly impossible feat. Taking a shower was something akin to climbing Mount Everest. *You don't have to do anything today,* I told myself. *Just put your feet on the floor.* Next—*You don't even have to take a step—just stand up.* Next—*You can stay in your pajamas—just walk to the bathroom and brush your teeth.* Like Anna stuck in the caverns of her despair, I wasn't able to look too far ahead. I was, however, able to trick my mind and body into doing one thing at a time. *I just have to look at my calendar for the day. In this moment, I simply have to send one email.* One step at a time. Before you know it, I might have actually gotten through the day.

This technique stuck with me when I was in any state of mental health, teaching me that clarity isn't magically found. Just like passion, creativity, or any other abstract entity, we don't manifest clarity by nebulously chasing it. Clarity is created and built, one step at a time.

My journey since I quit my job is one extreme case study of this concept. When we feel stuck in a lack of clarity, we often think we have to take some big action to get unstuck. Quit the job. Travel the world. Write the book. All of these things seem like huge decisions, and rightly so. They were leaps and bounds away from the possibilities I thought were attainable for myself.

These decisions, however, weren't made clear to me until I took an active step toward something. I only arrived to quitting my job after I allowed myself to explore beyond my day-to-day routine, seek other opportunities, and pursue my own interests in Costa Rica. I didn't have a six-month itinerary around the United States, China, and Europe; I simply allowed myself to follow my intuition. This book happened one idea at a time, one page at a time.

In uprooting my entire life to apply these concepts in large ways, I found that the method works with almost anything, small or large. There's a reason why compound interest works. Little actions, done repeatedly, add up to much bigger results, even if we cannot see what those results might be yet.

Want to start running? Put on your shoes.

Always wanted to learn how to draw? Pick up a pencil.

Behind on your reading goal for the year? Read one page.

Want to look for another job? Reach out to one person you could talk to.

Want to start a company? Talk so someone about a problem they have.

Do something, anything, besides passively scroll on your phone.

CHAPTER 9

DESIGN, TEST, ITERATE, REPEAT

The process is the reward. That's it.

—JONAH HILL

My gray T-shirt, high-rise jeans, and white leather shoes are all from the supposedly environmentally and socially conscious store, the one that always has a line wrapped outside the block on any given weekend in SoHo.

I do my laundry with the detergent from the shop with the billowy blue and white fabrics in the front window, the one where the sweet women at the counter look as clean and nontoxic as the white bottle they sold me.

I stand on the subway, soaking in the endless infomercial I am now starring in, just like Jim Carrey's character in the film *The Truman Show*.

The pastel-colored suitcases call my name, promising a home between homes.

The cool, linen sheets whisper that they will melt the stress away, providing only comfort and relaxation.

The sleek, metallic toothbrush swears it will bring delight to my daily routine.

Delight. Delight is the pinnacle of what a product strives to deliver. All of these products vow to bring me delight.

As my friend, designer and investor Tina He, writes, "The aspirational rhetoric of these brands has helped me name my own needs that I did not know I have. I've found it much easier to have a conversation intellectualizing the optimal best practice of 'self-help' rather than talking about my own emotions."[65]

Outsourcing emotions to products is nothing new. Coca Cola has been doing it for over a century. Its very first ad ran in the *Atlanta Journal* newspaper on May 29, 1886, promising to be "Delicious! Refreshing! Exhilarating! Invigorating!" Starting in 1929, "The Pause That Refreshes" was used for almost three decades. More recently, "Open Happiness" ran in 2009 and "Taste the Feeling" swept movie theaters around the world starting in 2016.[66]

---

65 Tina He, "Meaning Finding on the Internet," *Fakepixels*, May 9, 2020.
66 Ted Ryan, "Coca-Cola slogans through the years," *Coca-Cola*, February 27, 2019.

The only difference with these modern brands is that most of them utilize the direct-to-consumer (DTC) approach. Without any third-party distributors or middlemen of retailers, these digital-first brands center everything on the end consumer. As customers, we love feeling important and understood, which in turn leads to brand loyalty. With trustworthy names such as Oscar, Casper, and Marcus, these businesses seamlessly integrate into our lives. We reference them in speech as nonchalantly as the name of a roommate or pet.[67]

On the job, I utilized the same process of focusing on the end user to design financial systems. Off the job, I ignored this process and mindlessly consumed commodified versions of empty promises.

After I quit, the only end customer in my life was myself.

If I'm a product manager, I think, *I might as well manage my life.*

***

Empathize. Define. Ideate. Prototype. Test.

I, along with thirty other first-year engineering students, learned the design thinking process as the foundation of all our work. From designing a device to correctly perform squats to gamifying curriculum for better learning engagement, we applied design thinking to it all.

---

67 Janine Wolf, "Marcus, Casper, Oscar: Why Startups Are Obsessed With Human Names," *Bloomberg*, June 6, 2018.

Two years later, the same professor taught another design class, in which I was introduced to the book *Designing Your Life* by Bill Burnett and Dave Evans. These two Silicon Valley innovators created the most popular class at Stanford University, applying the design thinking mantra to build a well-lived, joyful life.[68] I ended up embracing the process so much that I taught a "Designing Your Life" seminar myself to twelve engineering majors the semester before I graduated.

In the world of design, technology, and entrepreneurship, the concept of minimum viable product (MVP) is widely referenced. Eric Ries, author of *The Lean Startup,* popularized the term in 2009, defining MVP as "that version of a new product which allows a team to collect the maximum amount of validated learning about customers with the least effort."[69]

Instead of creating a fully developed product requiring a ton of resources before it gets put in front of people who will be using it, the MVP is used to test reactions and interest so that there is more flexibility to change. Money and time are often saved, while also assuring that people will indeed use and enjoy what is produced.

At an event held in the Buzzfeed office, I listened to a speaker visualize the MVP model with circles. A single circle in the middle represented the core function of the product. Without this core feature, there would be no product. Adding features would be adding rings around the middle circle, each

---

68 William Burnett and David John Evans, *Designing Your Life: How to Build a Well-lived, Joyful Life* (New York: Alfred A. Knopf, 2016).
69 Eric Ries, "Minimum Viable Product: a guide," *Startup Lessons Learned,* August 3, 2009.

complete with its own design and testing phase. Equipped with the aesthetic essentials of clear-framed glasses and the Brooklyn hipster beard, he preached on how each concentric circle pointed the product closer to its North Star, the mission of it all.

The MVP concept is also often depicted in the form of a pyramid, going from bottom to top with four layers, reminiscent of Maslow's hierarchy of needs. These layers are typically labeled as *functional, reliable, usable, and delightful,* core buckets of requirements for product design and development.[70]

Traditional, antiquated design processes go up the pyramid, needing to achieve functionality before reliability, reliability before usability, and usability before delight. The MVP model, however, aims to design a prototype to include a slice of all four layers at a time, going from left to right. This way, each phase includes a slice of all four requirements, able to be tested at each level.

What if we were thinking of Maslow's hierarchy as the antiquated way, thinking we had to go up the pyramid over the course of life when we actually could slice our lives from left to right? Perhaps I didn't need to put my head down for two years while completely ignoring psychological and self-fulfillment needs. Perhaps I could spend my time building MVPs across the pyramid, testing to see what worked and what didn't.

---

70 Brian Pagán, "Lean Startup MVP: How To Make Meaningful Products," *Be. Human.*, updated February 25, 2019.

Applying product theory to personal development isn't anything new. We've done this with applying metrics of success and key performance indicators (KPI) to any goals regarding grades, health, or salary. If I wasn't careful, I knew I could fall into the trap of the traditionally quantified life measured on numbers of efficiency and productivity. Instead of this results-based nature, I focused my efforts on my mantra of the *process* of design thinking and product development.

What was my North Star? How is Amy defined at the core of the MVP, without any of the fluffy features? How could I set up experiments to safely test my dreams? How could I reflect, reiterate, and try again? How could I reframe adversity and failure to be simply part of the larger experiment?

There is only one thing that makes a dream impossible to achieve: the fear of failure.
             −PAULO COELHO, THE ALCHEMIST

Coupled with fear of judgment and not being good enough, failure is one of the steps in the experimental process that I have the most trouble with.

Sara Blakely, self-made billionaire and the founder of Spanx, is a testament to the power of reframing failure. I had always heard of Spanx and vaguely knew Blakely's origin story, but never bought a pair or really looked into it because I was never interested in the product for myself. After watching an empowering episode featuring Sara Blakely and Reese Witherspoon on the show *Shine On with Reese*, I was so hooked that I almost went online to buy a pair of Spanx, just to see what the long-lasting hype was about.

The biggest lesson I learned from Sara Blakely is one of learning how to reframe failure into an opportunity for character development. Since she was really little, her dad would ask both her and her brother at the dinner table what they had failed at that week. He'd be disappointed if there was nothing to be said. She remembers one night she came home and exclaimed, "Dad, Dad, I tried out for this and it was horrible!" Her dad then gave her a high five and said, "Way to go!" She didn't realize it at the time, but her dad was completely redefining failure in her life. True failure for her brother and her wasn't about the outcome—it was about not trying.[71]

On the talk show, Reese responds in amazement, as I did when I watched it. Reese then goes on to say how there are days that she's so on it, on fire getting everything done, and then there are days where she only feels 30 percent of herself, as if she's "lobotomized." What shifted her perspective to those 30 percent days is when she was in a movie in which she was playing a softball player, and a coach said to her, "I don't care if you have 30 percent, just give me 100 percent of that 30 percent." Looking at Sara, Reese throws up her hands and exclaims, "Thank you. What a relief. Permission to not be perfect."

On screen, when Reese and Sara bonded over the myth of perfection that so many people, especially women, are

---

71 *Shine On with Reese,* directed by Reese Witherspoon, Season 1, episode 5, "Sara Blakely, Candace Nelson," aired July 17, 2018, on Netflix.

trapped in, I couldn't help but think of my own relationship to perfectionism. Between seventh grade and tenth grade, I had a "Project Perfect" plan in my notes, meticulously spelling out every minute of my day and what I could or could not do. I never executed it very well, but that didn't stop me from planning. In middle school, people would refer to me as "Perfect Amy," marveling if I made anything less than a ninety-five out of one hundred. External expectations fueled my internal drive, and I continued to self-sabotage true action by putting a million different things on my plate and procrastinating everything I did.

I learned to take failure in stride throughout my life, but I never sought it out like Sara. Though I rationally knew about the importance of failing forward, I never fully internalized it. Sara's philosophy is to look at all the things she's afraid of—embarrassment, failure, others' opinions—and goes straight toward them.

What if all kids were brought up this way, instead of being fixated on achievement, grades, and perfection? How much more would we be willing to try, to take risks, to put ourselves out there with potentially world-changing ideas? Sara Blakely's story is one example of where this mindset was the key to her success.

When Sara was sixteen years old, she went through one of the darkest times in her life. Not only was one of her friends run over by a car in front of her, but at almost the exact same time, her parents were going through a separation. Her dad, as he was leaving, came into her bedroom and handed her a cassette tape series on affirmations and manifestation. She always had it playing in her car in high school, and no one wanted to be stuck in her car. After every party, people would say, "Do not go home with Sara 'cause she's gonna make you listen to that crap." Fast forward twenty years: When she ended up on the cover of *Forbes,* her phone blew up with texts from people from Clearwater High that said, "Damn, I should've listened to that s--t."[72]

Early in her life, she originally had her ambitions set on being a trial attorney, following in the footsteps of her father. She participated in debate in high school and college, where she majored in legal communications. However, she completely bombed the LSAT. Being no stranger to failure, she poured herself into studying, signed up for a prep course, and took another shot at the test—only to score one point worse.[73]

***

Think about it—if Sara Blakely had not failed the LSAT, not only once but *twice,* Spanx would not have been born, and she most likely would not have become the billionaire entrepreneur she is today.

In response to her defeat, she went to work for the happiest place on Earth, Disney World. "In my mind, the universe was now telling me to drive to Disney World and audition for the role of Goofy," Blakely said. However, Disney World

---

[72] Ibid.
[73] Gillian Zoe Segal, "This self-made billionaire failed the LSAT twice, then sold fax machines for 7 years before hitting big—here's how she got there," *CNBC,* April 3, 2019.

only held auditions for the character roles every once in a while, so in the meantime she got a job at Epcot.[74]

She finally got her chance to try out to be Goofy but was told that she was "too short to wear the costume." They gave her the role of a chipmunk instead, but according to Disney policy, she couldn't transition into it until she stayed in her initially employed role for a period of time. So, she continued to wear her brown polyester spacesuit and put people on Epcot rides until she got tired of it and went back home to live with her mother.

Having to pivot from law and Goofy, Sara started selling fax machines door to door for a company that "was the kind of place that would hire anyone with a pulse." On her first day, they handed her a phone book and told her, "Here are your four zip codes. Now get out there and sell." Sara relayed, "There was no list of accounts that were likely to buy from me. I had to 100 percent drum up my own leads. Waking up early to drive around cold calling from 8 a.m. to 5 p.m., most doors were slammed in my face. I saw my business card ripped up at least once a week, and I even had a few police escorts out of buildings."

She never let her miserable job get to her and instead found growth and amusement from it. Day in and day out, she started getting the nagging feeling that she wasn't in the right life. After the thought *This is not my life, what happened?* was too strong to fight, she went home that night and wrote down, "I want to invent my own product that I can sell to

---

74 Ibid.

millions of people that will make them feel good." Then she looked up and said, "Universe—give me the idea, and I will not squander it."

Many of us are familiar with the Spanx origin story that happened afterward. She couldn't find the right underwear to wear underneath her fitted white pants, so she cut the feet out of a pair of pantyhose and substituted them for underwear. With this makeshift pantyhose turned underwear, she was able to benefit from the fitting shape while still letting her feet go bare with her sandals. In creating a solution for her own problem, Sara also found the idea that answered her prayers. She said, "The moment I saw how good my butt looked, I was like, 'Thank you, God, this is my opportunity!'"[75]

Thus, Spanx was born, a new type of body undergarment that was comfortable, thin, and invisible under clothing. With only $5,000 and no borrowing or outside money, she bootstrapped Spanx from her apartment. You can now find Spanx all over the world. During a layover in the Atlanta airport, I saw the shiny gemstone letters on the deep red storefront, wondering if Sara Blakely had any idea what she would create back in those moments.

She says it was only because she previously spoke the affirmation of wanting to invent her own product that she even recognized she had an idea, let alone had the courage to run with it.[76] It wasn't necessarily the idea itself, but the openness and willingness her mind and heart were predisposed

---

[75] Gillian Zoe Segal, "This self-made billionaire failed the LSAT twice, then sold fax machines for 7 years before hitting big—here's how she got there."
[76] Ibid.

to already. Sara Blakely proves that running toward failure, despite fear, is worth the risk. Coupled with the courage to dream big, using failure as a testing grounds and not an end result allows you to carve a path beyond what you may have thought possible.

CHAPTER 10

MIRRORS BEYOND OURSELVES

Friends hold a mirror up to each other; through that mirror they can see each other in ways that would not otherwise be accessible to them, and it is this mirroring that helps them improve themselves as persons.

—ARISTOTLE

Shivering from the cold, I take off my gloves, hat, and coat as I enter the bakery. Ordering a simple oatmeal bowl with fruit, I settle onto a seat at the bar counter—perfect for solo travelers like me who are dining alone.

A couple moments later, a woman comes in, looks around for an empty spot, and sits right next to me. Chatting comfortably with the server in German, I can tell she is local to Austria. She smiles at me hesitantly, motioning whether it's okay to put her scarf and mittens next to me on the table.

We start making small talk. She introduces herself as Sofia. She asks where I'm visiting from, and I ask if she lives in Vienna. "I grew up an hour outside of town," she says. "I'm a psychotherapist, so I'm only in the city for a couple of days for a psychology conference."

Since we're in a raw, vegan bakery, we discuss the food and our respective diets. She shares how she feels so much healthier overall from eating a plant-based diet. "You know," she states as she munches on her oatmeal, "food is so connected to emotions, whether it's comfort food, eating chocolate or sweets when we're sad, or breaking bread together as a connection to others."

Sofia's face lights up as she talks about this. Clearly, it's a topic she's thought about a lot. She continues to tell me how she woke up with a thought that morning about how food is used as an excuse to be with people. Pausing for a moment to eat a bite of toast, she states, "People always need some barrier—whether it's eating or drinking or smoking or clubbing or coffee." We discuss various buffers that act as social lubricants and how hanging out just to be together is rare across many cultures. "That's too dangerous," she shakes her head. "People don't know what to do if there's nothing between them."

I ask her what she thinks people are scared about. "I don't know. It's like we're in a river with a stick in the middle, and we need that stick of safety to hold onto. If we let go, we could drown." She shares this description as I mull over the visual in my head. *We're scared of drowning in our own vulnerability.*

"The ironic part is that we need this river to get through life. We need other people to show us our fears." With that, she gets up abruptly and returns her tray. Piling on her mittens and scarf, she takes a few steps toward the door before turning back, saying, "Thank you for showing me my fear."

Don't tell someone to be resilient; instead, create an environment where resilience is possible. Create an environment where resilience is inevitable.

–EMILY SANTIAGO

"That sounds like a personal problem," is something we often hear or think in response to issues surrounding emotions, feelings, and mental health.

Personal development, personal growth, self-help, whatever you want to call it, is not an isolated activity. While we look inward as much as possible, only in the context of others can we truly transform. Friendship is one way we can hold up mirrors to one another. Community is another. Through relationships with others, we are able to understand ourselves and grow in different ways.

We often hear of how social support can increase longevity and even prevent dementia. One study found that "lack of strong relationships increased the risk of premature death from all causes by 50 percent—an effect on mortality risk roughly comparable to smoking up to fifteen cigarettes a day, and greater than obesity and physical inactivity."[77]

I recently participated in an event titled "Burnout Is a Community Issue, Not an Individual One," held by educational psychologist Emily Santiago. She explained to us how trauma isn't isolated and in fact impacts everything around us. Likewise, it is the onus of the collective to be there for each other.

At any given moment, we belong in various parts of the ecosystem. Emily presented her "dynamic empowerment matrix," which states that depending on our own levels of resilience and trauma, we're able to be empowered, empower ourselves, empower others, or seek empowerment from others. She emphasized how we cycle through these phases throughout time, and no quadrant is any "better" than the other. Asking for help is just as important as giving help.

Being a part of a community allows us to create soft landings for each other when we fall. At the same time, we can also be there to lift each other up and go to places we couldn't have reached on our own.

---

77 Julianne Holt-Lunstad, Timothy B Smith, and Bradley J Layton, "Social Relationships and Mortality Risk: A Meta-analytic Review". *PLoS Med* 7, no. 7 (July 27, 2010): e1000316.

When you get these jobs that you have been so brilliantly trained for, just remember that your real job is that if you are free, you need to free somebody else. If you have some power, then your job is to empower somebody else.

–TONI MORRISON

When I announced to my coworkers that I was leaving, I was honest in telling them that I was taking a break and wanted to explore different interests, one of which was environmental sustainability. They knew from me gently asking about their plastic water bottles and dropping off compost during lunch breaks that I cared a lot about the climate crisis.

During my last week at the office, one of the software engineers on my team came around to my desk. He asked, "Amy, do you have to leave? It's not just the environment out there that needs you; this environment needs you, too."

His comment stuck with me wherever I went. I realized that to effectively care for *any* environment beyond myself, I had to care for my internal environment first. All of my classes in sustainability taught the issue as holistic, touching on every single system that exists, but I hadn't fully grasped it. When I felt personally burnt out, I didn't have the energy to care enough about the planet burning out. Even little things like recycling felt like pointless efforts, let alone thinking about greater policy or action I could partake in.

The ideas of "putting on your own oxygen mask first before helping others" or "you can't pour from an empty cup" are becoming trite phrases when emphasizing the importance of self-care. However, I've noticed that the more we focus on self-care, the more we stop the conversation there. We forget that we care for ourselves in hopes that we are able to push our capacity to care beyond ourselves. We do this inner work so that we are able to show up as better humans in the external world.

Consider this a call to action—yes, for yourself, but also beyond yourself. I hope we can continue to show up and do the work together.

FINAL THOUGHTS

I am no longer accepting the things I cannot change. I am changing the things I cannot accept.

–ANGELA DAVIS

Several months into my job, I decided I didn't want to be someone who complained about where they were and didn't do anything about it. I reminded myself that I chose my work, my path, and my environment. Once I shifted into this perspective, I was able to enjoy my day to day. Instead of putting my hands up and surrendering completely to the negative talk around me, I changed my mindset around the situation and decided to make the best of it.

There's an expression that goes, "Bloom where you are planted." I love this quote because it signifies that people are able to thrive wherever they are. For the first period of my life, this quote worked, as I didn't embrace personal agency. Now that I take ownership of my own life, I'd like to replace "bloom" with "choose." *Choose where you are planted.*

Deciding to no longer procrastinate in living life leads me to see things in a different light. I actively choose what I give time, attention, and energy to. I write beautiful stories about watching the sunrise, playing with my niece, and reading by the fireplace. I give my body time and space to rest and heal, knowing I will be more prepared for whatever comes my way.

I wrote this book during a special time in not only my own life, but also during a unique time throughout the entire globe. The Greek word apocalypse means, "uncovering" or "revealing." As I was going through a personal uncovering of emotions, burnout, and mental health, the world was also going through a collective apocalypse from a worldwide pandemic.

I didn't know that while writing it, I'd be relying on practices of mindfulness, emotional awareness, and effective action to help myself and others manage our well-being in real time.

I didn't know that I'd meditate with people from Sweden, Germany, Italy, Indonesia, and Australia every single day for a month to help make sense of what was happening.

I didn't know that I'd hold mindfulness sessions with my best friend who had COVID-19 and how much she'd contribute feeling better to the breathwork we did together.

I didn't know that there would be a massive uncovering of horrific racial injustice toward Black lives and how much more I'd realize that both inner and outer work matters in order to build more equitable and just environments for all.

This book is a meditation of the past year, containing the stories I told myself and the stories I heard from others. My wish is that it will help you embrace your own uncovering to reclaim control.

ACKNOWLEDGMENTS

To my family, my mom, dad, Gloria, and Anna—thank you for your unconditional love, patience, and understanding.

To the friends who hold up a mirror to help me see what I cannot myself—I am grateful.

To Dig Well readers—thank you for making me feel like my writing matters.

To the Jack Kent Cooke Foundation—thank you for supporting me to dream big from an early age and for giving me an extended family. Thank you especially to Jennifer Bockman, my educational adviser, for encouraging me over a decade ago that I could achieve my long-term goal of writing a book.

To the New Degree Press team, especially Eric Koester, Brian Bies, Linda Berardelli, and Melody Delgado Lorbeer—this would not have been possible without your guidance, expertise, and commitment.

To my early supporters—thank you for believing in me. I could not have done this without you all:

Aakash B	Daisy U
Aaron M	Daksh B
Adam E	Dalianna V
Alanna S	Danial H
Albert C	Emily A
Alex W	Emily R
Alicia W	Gabby O
Amanda C	Gabrielle R
Amanda W	Hannah W
Amanullah W	Jackie K
Amit P	Jacob H
Andrew L	Jaime L
Andrew T	James C
Angelica F	Jason H
Ann McClain B	Jenny E
Anthony C	Jessica T
Anvar S	Jimmy Y
Arthur D	Jiwon L
Audrey F	John D
Ben M	Jong Rim M
Biruktawit A	Joy F
Cameron W	Katie G
Caroline B	Kenneth M
Chelsea H	Kevin P
Cheng X	Kyle L
Chris L	Lauren F
Cleo C	Leidy K
Cliff M	Leila M
Crystal E	LeiLei S

Linda M
Lubnah A
MacKenzie H
Madison D
Mani C
Maria M
Mariana G
Martín G
Matt D
Meenakshi S
Megan G
Meiya C
Melanie G
Michelle L
Michelle W
Natnael K
Neeka K
Nick K
Nilesh P
Orpheas K
Owen C
Patric C
Patrick S
Paul M
Penny X
Perrin F
Peyton A
Rachel S
Radhika K
Ramiro B
Reilly S
Ronald D

Ryan D
Sara M
Sarika P
Scott D
Shota O
Simran P
Soobin O
Sophia C
Suhaib R
Tim M
Tyler C
Virginia D
Wei L
Winnie T
Ximena P
Yash T
Yoojin K
Yoshmar P
Yuesen H
Yujing L

APPENDIX

INTRODUCTION

Africa, Jei and Majose Carrasco. "Asian-American and Pacific Islander Mental Health." *National Alliance on Mental Illness*, February 2011. http://www.drjeiafrica.com/Dr._Jei_Africa/Media_files/NAMIAAPI.pdf

Agrawal, Sangeeta and Ben Wigert. "Employee Burnout, Part 1: The 5 Main Causes." *Gallup,* July 12, 2018. https://www.gallup.com/workplace/237059/employee-burnout-part-main-causes.aspx

Helliwell, John F., Richard Layard, and Jeffrey D. Sachs. "World Happiness Report 2019." *Sustainable Development Solutions Network.* March 20, 2019. https://worldhappiness.report/ed/2019/

Patriot Act. "Hasan Hears Hot Takes From The Audience | Deep Cuts | Patriot Act with Hasan Minhaj | Netflix." December 19, 2019. Video, 19:11. https://www.youtube.com/watch?v=sYS-hB-DzYO8

CHAPTER 1

Gale, Catharine R, G David Batty, and Ian J Deary. "Locus of Control at Age 10 Years and Health Outcomes and Behaviors at Age 30 Years: The 1970 British Cohort Study." *Psychosom Med* 70, no. 4 (May 2008): 397-403. https://doi.org/10.1097/psy.0b013e31816a719e

Hoehn-Saric, R and D R Mcleod. "Locus of Control in Chronic Anxiety Disorders." *Acta psychiatrica Scandinavica* 72, no. 6 (December 1985): 529-35. https://doi.org/10.1111/j.1600-0447.1985.tb02650.x

Joelson, Richard B. "Locus of Control." *Psychology Today*, August 2, 2017. https://www.psychologytoday.com/us/blog/moments-matter/201708/locus-control

CHAPTER 2

"First Destination Report: Class of 2019." *Yale University, Office of Career Strategy*, 2019. https://ocs.yale.edu/sites/default/files/files/OCS%20Stats%20pages/Final%20Class%20of%202019%20Report.pdf

Franck, Thomas W. "The Graduating Class of 2017 by the numbers." *The Harvard Crimson*, May 2017. https://features.thecrimson.com/2017/senior-survey/after-harvard-narrative/index.html

Harter, Jim. "Employee Engagement on the Rise in the U.S." *Gallup*, August 26, 2018. https://news.gallup.com/poll/241649/employee-engagement-rise.aspx

Keegan, Marina. "Even artichokes have doubts." *Yale Daily News,* September 30, 2011. https://yaledailynews.com/blog/2011/09/30/even-artichokes-have-doubts/

Klein, Ezra. "Anand Giridharadas on the elite charade of changing the world." September 5, 2018. In *Vox.* Podcast, 01:35:48.

https://www.vox.com/2018/9/5/17821522/anand-giridharadas-winner-take-all-ezra-klein-podcast

Sofian, Indra. "How Top-Performing College Grads Fall Into the 'Prestige Career' Trap." *Medium,* January 21, 2019. https://medium.com/s/story/a-culture-of-prestige-98c8671ceade

Wissner-Gross, Elizabeth. *What High Schools Don't Tell You: 300+ Secrets to Make Your Kid Irresistible to Colleges by Senior Year.* New York: Penguin Group, 2007.

CHAPTER 3

Baila, Morgan. "How Does *Mean Girls*' Most Iconic Scene Hold Up Today? We Asked 5 Real Teens." *Refinery29,* April 30, 2019. https://www.refinery29.com/en-us/2019/04/230395/mean-girls-cafeteria-map-cliques-racist-stereotypes

Hook, Leslie. "'People love the Uber product; they don't necessarily love the brand'". *Financial Times,* December 6, 2017. https://www.ft.com/content/0fefb486-da16-11e7-a039-c64b1c09b482

Parker, Priya. *The Art of Gathering: How We Meet and why it Matters.* New York: Riverhead Books, 2018.

Parker, Priya. "Sustained Dialogue: How Students Are Changing Their Own Racial Climate." *About Campus* 11, no. 1 (March-April 2006): 17-23. https://sdatuva.files.wordpress.com/2010/09/sustained-dialogue-how-students-are-changing-their-own-racial-climate.pdf

Veerasamy, Visakan. *friendly ambitious nerd*. Self-published, Gumroad, 2020.

Waters, Mark, dir. *Mean Girls*. Paramount Pictures, 2004. Film.

Welteroth, Elaine. *More Than Enough: Claiming Space for Who You Are (No Matter What They Say)*. New York: Viking, 2019.

CHAPTER 4

Gottlieb, Lori. *Maybe You Should Talk to Someone: A Therapist, HER Therapist, and Our Lives Revealed*. New York: HMH Books, 2019.

Kam, Brandt, Hadrian Mendoza, and Akihiko Masuda. "Mental Health Help-Seeking Experience and Attitudes in Latina/o American, Asian American, Black American, and White American College Students." *International Journal for the Advancement of Counselling* 41 (2019): 492-508. https://doi.org/10.1007/s10447-018-9365-8

Lipson, Sarah Ketchen, Emily G. Lattie, and Daniel Eisenberg. "Increased Rates of Mental Health Service Utilization by U.S. College Students: 10-Year Population-Level Trends (2007–2017)." *Psychiatric Services* 70, no. 1 (January 1, 2019): 60-63. https://doi.org/10.1176/appi.ps.201800332

"Low Hemoglobin." *Cleveland Clinic,* Updated February 2, 2018. https://my.clevelandclinic.org/health/symptoms/17705-low-hemoglobin

Stebleton, Michael J., Krista M. Soria, and Ronald L. Huesman. "First-generation students' sense of belonging, mental health, and use of counseling services at public research universities." *Journal of College Counseling* 17, no. 1 (April 2014): 6-20. https://doi.org/10.1002/j.2161-1882.2014.00044.x

"The Deteriorating Mental Health of U.S. College Students: Part I." *Imagine America,* March 2, 2020. https://www.imagine-america.org/deteriorating-mental-health-u-s-college-students-part/

CHAPTER 5

Ben-Shahar, Tal. *Happier: learn the secrets to daily joy and lasting fulfillment.* New York: McGraw-Hill, 2007.

Golkar, A., E. Johansson, M. Kasahara, W. Osika, A. Perski, and I. Savic. "The influence of work-related chronic stress on the regulation of emotion and on functional connectivity in the brain." *PLoS ONE* 9, no 9 (September 3, 2014): e104550. https://doi.org/10.1371/journal.pone.0104550

King, Noel. "When A Psychologist Succumbed To Stress, He Coined The Term 'Burnout'." December 8, 2016. In *Planet Money NPR.* Podcast, 3:00. https://www.npr.org/2016/12/08/504864961/when-a-psychologist-succumbed-to-stress-he-coined-the-term-burnout

Leiter, Michael P. and Christina Maslach. "Six Areas of Worklife: A Model of the Organizational Context of Burnout." *Journal of Health and Human Services Administration* 21. no 4 (Spring 1999): 472-489. https://pubmed.ncbi.nlm.nih.gov/10621016/

Petersen, Anne Helen. "Here's What "Millennial Burnout" Is Like For 16 Different People." *Buzzfeed News,* January 9, 2019. https://www.buzzfeednews.com/article/annehelenpetersen/millennial-burnout-perspectives

Petersen, Anne Helen. "How Millennials Became The Burnout Generation." *Buzzfeed News,* January 5, 2019. https://www.buzzfeednews.com/article/annehelenpetersen/millennials-burnout-generation-debt-work

Saturday Night Live. "Romano Tours." May 4, 2019, Video, 4:11. https://www.youtube.com/watch?v=TbwlC2B-BIg

Saunders, Elizabeth Grace. "To Recover from Burnout, Regain Your Sense of Control." *Harvard Business Review,* December 5, 2017. https://hbr.org/2017/12/to-recover-from-burnout-regain-your-sense-of-control

Savic, I. "Structural changes of the brain in relation to occupational stress." *Cerebral Cortex* 25, no. 6 (June 2015): 1554–1564. https://doi.org/10.1093/cercor/bht348

Seneca, Lucius Annaeus. *Letters from a Stoic: Volume I.* Translated by Richard Mott Gummere. Enhanced Media, 2016.

Yeo, Lawrence. "Travel Is No Cure for the Mind." *More To That*, March 21, 2019. https://medium.com/personal-growth/travel-is-no-cure-for-the-mind-e449d3109d71

CHAPTER 6

Haidt, Jonathan. *The Happiness Hypothesis: Finding Modern Truth in Ancient Wisdom*. New York: Basic Books, 2006.

Kabat-Zinn, John. "Mindfulness-Based Interventions in Context: Past, Present, and Future." *Clinical Psychology Science and Practice* 10, no. 2 (June 2003): 144-156. https://doi.org/10.1093/clipsy.bpg016

Urban, Tim. "Why Procrastinators Procastinate." *Wait But Why*, October 30, 2013. https://waitbutwhy.com/2013/10/why-procrastinators-procrastinate.html

CHAPTER 7

Brach, Tara. "The Wisdom of "It's Not My Fault": Finding Freedom When We are Caught in Self-Blame." *Tara Brach*, August 9, 2017. http://blog.tarabrach.com/2017/08/the-wisdom-of-its-not-my-fault-finding.html

Brackett, Marc. *Permission to Feel: Unlocking the Power of Emotions to Help Our Kids, Ourselves, and Our Society Thrive*. Celadon Books, 2019.

Brown, Brené. *The Gifts of Imperfection: Let Go of Who You Think You're Supposed to Be and Embrace Who You Are*. Minnesota: Hazelden Publishing, 2010.

Byron, Katie. "The Work is a Practice." *The Work of Byron Katie.* Updated 2020. https://thework.com/instruction-the-work-byron-katie/

Gerald, Casey. *There Will Be No Miracles Here: A Memoir.* New York: Penguin Publishing Group, 2018.

Laporte, Danielle. *The Desire Map: A Guide to Creating Goals with Soul.* Sounds True, 2014.

Luse, Brittany and Eric Eddings. "You Don't Make Free People."August 15, 2009. In *The Nod.* Podcast, 52:00. https://gimletmedia.com/shows/the-nod/mehak5

CHAPTER 8

Doyle, Glennon. *Untamed.* New York: Random House Publishing Group, 2020.

Garcia-Navarro, Lulu and Emma Bowman. "For 'Frozen II,' Kristen Bell Found Inspiration In Personal Pain." *NPR,* December 8, 2019. https://www.npr.org/2019/12/08/785530098/for-frozen-ii-kristen-bell-found-inspiration-in-personal-pain

Grohol, John M. "What is Exposure Therapy?" *PsychCentral,* October 8, 2018. https://psychcentral.com/lib/what-is-exposure-therapy/

Lee, Jennifer and Chris Buck, dir. *Frozen II.* 2019; Burbank, CA: Walt Disney Pictures. Film.

Maier, Steven F. and Martin E. P. Seligman. "Learned Helplessness at Fifty: Insights forom Neuroscience." *Psychol Rev.* 123, no. 4 (July 2016): 349-367. https://dx.doi.org/10.1037%2Frev0000033

Seligman, Martin E. and Steven F. Maier. "Failure to escape traumatic shock." *Journal of Experimental Psychology* 74, no. 1 (1967): 1-9. https://psycnet.apa.org/doi/10.1037/h0024514

van der Kolk, Bessel. *The Body Keeps the Score: Brain, Mind, and Body in the Healing of Trauma.* New York: Penguin Books, 2015.

van der Kolk, Bessel and Ruth Buczynski. "Four Concrete Steps for Working with Trauma." *New York Association of Psychiatric Rehabilitation,* November 18, 2015. https://www.nyaprs.org/e-news-bulletins/2015/bessel-van-der-kolk-four-concrete-steps-for-working-with-trauma

CHAPTER 9

Burnett, William and David John Evans. *Designing Your Life: How to Build a Well-lived, Joyful Life.* New York: Alfred A. Knopf, 2016.

He, Tina. "Meaning Finding on the Internet." *Fakepixels,* May 9, 2020. https://fakepixels.substack.com/p/fkpxls-vol41-meaning-finding-on-the

McLeod, Saul. "Maslow's Hierarchy of Needs." *Simply Psychology,* Updated March 20, 2020. https://www.simplypsychology.org/maslow.html

Pagán, Brian. "Lean Startup MVP: How To Make Meaningful Products." *Be. Human.*, Updated February 25, 2019. https://brianpagan.net/2015/lean-startup-mvp-how-to-make-meaningful-products/

Ries, Eric. "Minimum Viable Product: a guide." *Startup Lessons Learned*, August 3, 2009. http://www.startuplessonslearned.com/2009/08/minimum-viable-product-guide.html

Ryan, Ted. "Coca-Cola slogans through the years." *Coca-Cola*, February 27, 2019. https://www.coca-colacompany.com/au/news/coca-cola-slogans-through-the-years

Segal, Gillian Zoe. "This self-made billionaire failed the LSAT twice, then sold fax machines for 7 years before hitting big—here's how she got there." *CNBC*, April 3, 2019. https://www.cnbc.com/2019/04/03/self-made-billionaire-spanx-founder-sara-blakely-sold-fax-machines-before-making-it-big.html

Witherspoon, Reese, dir. *Shine on with Reese*. Season 1, episode 5, "Sara Blakely, Candace Nelson." Aired July 17, 2018, on Netflix.

Wolf, Janine. "Marcus, Casper, Oscar: Why Startups Are Obsessed With Human Names." *Bloomberg*, June 6, 2018. https://www.bloomberg.com/news/articles/2018-06-06/why-startups-keep-choosing-human-names

CHAPTER 10

Holt-Lunstad, Julianne, Timothy B Smith, and Bradley J Layton. "Social Relationships and Mortality Risk: A Meta-analytic Review". *PLoS Med* 7, no. 7 (July 27, 2010): e1000316. https://doi.org/10.1371/journal.pmed.1000316

Printed in Great Britain
by Amazon